Multilevel and Diverse Classrooms

Edited by Bradley Baurain and Phan Le Ha

Maria Dantas-Whitney, Sarah Rilling, and Lilia Savova, Series Editors

TESOL Classroom Practice Series

Typeset in ITC Galliard and Vag Rounded
by Capitol Communication Systems, Inc., Crofton, Maryland USA
Printed by United Graphics, Inc., Mattoon, Illinois USA
Indexed by Pueblo Indexing and Publishing Services, Pueblo West, Colorado USA

Teachers of English to Speakers of Other Languages, Inc.
1925 Ballenger Avenue, Suite 550
Alexandria, Virginia 22314 USA
Tel 703-836-0774 • Fax 703-836-6447 • E-mail tesol@tesol.org •
http://www.tesol.org/

Publishing Manager: Carol Edwards
Copy Editor: Sarah J. Duffy
Additional Reader: Terrey Hatcher
Cover Design: Capitol Communication Systems, Inc.

Every effort has been made to contact the copyright holders for permission to reprint
borrowed material. We regret any oversights that may have occurred and will rectify them
in future printings of this work.

All names of teachers, teacher learners, students, and places are pseudonyms or are used
with permission. Teacher and student work samples are used with permission.

The authors of chapter 5, "Every Student Wins: Using 'Team English' With Large, Multilevel Classes in Thailand," are extremely grateful to the students and their guardians for
the photographs used in the chapter. The Thailand-based author met with the children's
guardians and explained in Thai the need for consent to use the children's photos in the
published volume. However, the purpose and use of consent in U.S. publications has no
direct translation in the culture. The authors and TESOL, with due effort and in good
faith, have used only those photos for which they feel the permission was understood and
granted. No names or personal information of any student appears in the volume.

ISBN 9781931185653
Library of Congress Control No. 2009939648

Table of Contents

Spurring Creativity and Imagination

Expanding the Boundaries

Contents

Series Editors' Preface

The TESOL Classroom Practice Series showcases state-of-the-art curricula, materials, tasks, and activities reflecting emerging trends in language education and in the roles of teachers, learners, and the English language itself. The series seeks to build localized theories of language learning and teaching based on students' and teachers' unique experiences in and out of the classroom.

This series captures the dynamics of 21st-century English for speakers of other languages (ESOL) classrooms. It reflects major shifts in authority from teacher-centered practices to collaborative learner- and learning-centered environments. The series acknowledges the growing numbers of English speakers globally, celebrates locally relevant curricula and materials, and emphasizes the importance of multilingual and multicultural competencies—a primary goal in teaching English as an international language. Furthermore, the series takes into account contemporary technological developments that provide new opportunities for information exchange and social and transactional communications.

Each volume in the series focuses on a particular communicative skill, learning environment, or instructional goal. Chapters within each volume represent practices in English for general, academic, vocational, and specific purposes. Readers will find examples of carefully researched and tested practices designed for different student populations (from young learners to adults, from beginning to advanced) in diverse settings (from pre-K–12 to college and postgraduate, from local to global, from formal to informal). A variety of methodological choices are also represented, including individual and collaborative tasks and curricular as well as extracurricular projects. Most important, these volumes invite readers into the conversation that considers and so constructs ESOL classroom practices as complex entities. We are indebted to the authors, their colleagues, and their students for being a part of this conversation.

The benefits and advantages of classroom practices incorporating unity-in-diversity and diversity-in-unity are what *Multilevel and Diverse Classrooms* is all about. Multilevel classrooms—also known as mixed-ability or heterogeneous classrooms—are a fact of life in ESOL programs around the world. These classrooms are often not only multilevel but also large, multilingual, and multi-cultural. This volume adds to the growing knowledge base in language education of classroom practices in a variety of settings. Chapters in the volume approach multilevelness from a holistic and humanistic perspective by considering diversity not only in language skills and proficiencies, but also in learning styles, purposes, and contexts. The volume presents practices of teachers who thrive in multilevel classrooms and draw strength from unity.

> *Maria Dantas-Whitney, Western Oregon University*
> *Sarah Rilling, Kent State University*
> *Lilia Savova, Indiana University of Pennsylvania*

CHAPTER 1

The Multifaceted Classroom

Bradley Baurain and Phan Le Ha

A dying father in a Vietnamese folktale called his 10 children to his bedside. Handing the oldest son a stick of wood, the father invited him to break it. The son did so quite easily. Then the father handed him a bundle of 10 sticks and asked him to do it again. This time, no matter how hard the son exerted himself, he could not break even one of the sticks. The bundle remained intact. "Work together," the father advised his children, "and nothing can defeat you." This wise man wanted his family to understand the strength that flows from unity.

The benefits and advantages of unity-in-diversity and diversity-in-unity are what this book is all about. Multilevel classrooms—also known as mixed-ability or heterogeneous classrooms—are a fact of life in English to speakers of other languages (ESOL) programs around the world. They are often not only multilevel but also large, multilingual, and multicultural. For this reason, in this book we as coeditors approach multilevelness not solely as a technical issue involving instructional methods, classroom management, tasks, activities, and curriculum, though it certainly involves all of these (Baurain, 2005, 2007; Bell, 2004; Hess, 2001; Mathews-Aydinli & Van Horne, 2006; J. Rose, 1997). Rather, we approach the phenomenon of multilevelness from a holistic and humanistic perspective; our conception includes diversity not only in language skills and proficiencies, but also in learning styles, purposes, and contexts, including the sociocultural influences of ethnicity, gender, and other elements involved in the formation and development of learner and teacher identities (Phan, 2008). These and other factors contribute to the complexity and challenge of how we as teachers define and respond to groups of multilevel students.

By taking a more flexible and open-ended approach to the main topic of this volume, we are building bridges to work being done elsewhere in education (e.g., Hamann & Reeves, 2008; Schultz, 2003). We are also resisting the tendency of ESOL professional discourse to sound impersonal and mechanistic, as if we were programming language learning machines rather than working with people. Language acquisition is by no means as linear or predictable as a chemical reaction. Our stance prefers to embrace the inherent "messiness" of the learning process (see also Allwright, 2005; Oxford, Massey, & Anand, 2005).

It has been truthfully said that "all classes are mixed ability classes" (J. Rose, 1997, p. 3). Even when good placement tests or systems are in place, diversity among learners is inevitable. How are committed and creative teachers responding to this reality and benefiting their students? The chapters in this book represent answers from current classroom practice in a variety of settings. To make the contents applicable in other contexts—that is, transferable or generalizable in a broad sense—we are depending on dynamic reader interaction. You are the best judge of what is useful and relevant, and how and why, in your specific situation. In a sense, the father in the Vietnamese folktale had the easier job of pronouncing wisdom and passing on; it was the children left behind who had the harder task of putting his words into practice. We coeditors and chapter contributors will eventually close this volume and ride off into the sunset, as it were. It will be you who decide what to do, and how and why, with the bundle of sticks we offer here.

Multilevel and Diverse Classrooms is one volume in TESOL's Classroom Practice Series, one bundle of sticks within a larger bundle of sticks. As do the other volumes in the series, this book follows a consistent chapter template:

- Introduction
- Context
- Curriculum, Tasks, Materials
- Reflections

This structure helps unify the series as a whole and the chapters within this individual book, yet by scanning the table of contents one can see the great diversity in topics, contexts, and approaches. A variety of types of classrooms from around the world are also represented in this volume, including 4-year university, community college, P–12, teacher education, and adult education.

One additional note on this volume's approach to unity, diversity, and the multifaceted nature of teaching and learning ESOL concerns the presentation of contributors' names, including our own. The first coeditor's name is presented in the correct order, with family name (Baurain) last. The second coeditor's name is also presented in the correct order, with family name (Phan) first. Most chapter authors' names are listed in the same manner as the first coeditor, while the authors of chapter 14 are listed in the same manner as the second coeditor. Getting names right, we believe, is a small but important step toward achieving the kind of multilevel and diverse classrooms in which all of us can truly enjoy teaching and learning.

STANDING BEFORE A SEA OF FACES

This section groups four chapters set in contexts in which the ESOL classes are not only multilevel but also large (Hess, 2001; LoCastro, 2001). Chapter 2,

"Responding to the Challenge of Large Mixed-Ability Classes in China," by Alan Seaman, takes up the question of whether and how communicative and student-centered teaching principles formulated in one context (smaller classes, Western cultures) can be put into practice in other contexts (larger classes, non-Western cultures). Seaman narrates a sabbatical semester in China and critiques his pedagogical adaptations from a sociocultural and pragmatic perspective.

Chapter 3, "Large Classes and Group Projects: A Curriculum Unit on Tourism in the Philippines," by Doris H. Christopher and Roland A. Niez, is a multifaceted and multilayered account of project work, which is often recommended as a fruitful curricular approach within mixed-ability settings. The authors keep a variety of issues in focus and in balance, including small-group configurations, presentation and research skills, interpersonal dynamics, and motivating high- and low-proficiency learners alike.

Chapter 4, "Speaking in Crowds: Oral Activities for Large Classes With Few Resources," by Susan Donnelly Renaud, Elizabeth Tannenbaum, and Michael Jerald, is based on teacher training in Haiti and other environments where material classroom resources are scarce. The authors ask themselves, "What is a successful speaking activity?", and go on to craft guiding principles to answer this question for large multilevel classrooms and share five of their most productive activities.

Chapter 5, "Every Student Wins: Using 'Team English' With Large Multilevel Classes in Thailand," by Marguerite G. MacDonald and Ian L. Smith, describes a model based on a sports metaphor, right down to color-coded uniforms and a friendly spirit of competition. This model, which has been piloted and developed on the ground in Thailand, is a fresh take on small-group strategies that have long been employed in response to the challenge of multilevel classrooms. I (Brad) saw a demonstration of "Team English" at a recent Thailand TESOL Convention; the hundred or so participating teachers who jammed the room and left more excited than I have ever seen any group leave any conference session attest to the potential and success of this program.

SPURRING CREATIVITY AND IMAGINATION

This section includes five chapters that share an emphasis on visual and artistic resources. Chapter 6, "Go to Commercial: Using Television Commercials in Multilevel EFL Classrooms," by Frank Tuzi, Ann Junko Young, and Keiko Mori, discusses the effective use in mixed-ability environments of a widely available authentic form of text from the popular media: television commercials. The authors argue that these advertisements "provide not only jumping-off points for learning discrete linguistic and lexical items, but also an avenue for exploring culture and values" (p. 77).

Chapter 7, "Photography as a Cultural Text for Language Learning," by Walter Gene Pleisch and Joel See, begins with the anthropological and sociological tradition of photography as a research tool or means of gathering cultural artifacts and turns it into a language learning experience. The narrated project combines listening, speaking, reading, writing, collaborative learning, creativity, critical thinking, and environmental awareness.

Chapter 8, "iDeas for iPods in the Multilevel Language Classroom," by Troy Cox, Robb Mark McCollum, and Benjamin L. McMurry, taps into the contemporary phenomenon of MP3 players and considers how they might be used to meet language learning objectives. The authors' classroom-tested suggestions encompass taking advantage of these devices' audio, video, and text capabilities as well as using them for Web browsing, digital voice recording, and podcasting.

Chapter 9, "Teaching Smart, Using Art: Creativity at Work in Mixed-Ability Classes," by Linda M. Holden, highlights how and why stimulating learners' imaginations can benefit their language learning. The flexibility of her ideas for multilevel learners is demonstrated by means of two activities, one featuring a Calvin and Hobbes comic strip and the other a Norman Rockwell painting.

Chapter 10, "Online Comics: Writing, Reading, and Telling Stories in English," by Bill Zimmerman, features an online comics creation Web site that was also reviewed recently in *Essential Teacher* (Kirson, 2008). Using a library of characters, speech bubbles, and other tools created especially for literacy and ESOL programs, learners are invited to write and design their own comic strips. I (Brad) recall the first time I used this Web site with students in an intensive English program: In the computer lab, I handed out the assignment sheet, and students began to familiarize themselves with the site's resources. After several minutes, I also handed out a sample strip that involved a student's unbelievable excuse about undone homework and the teacher's humorous response. Students began chuckling, and the atmosphere lightened. It seemed as though my example freed them to write "something real." All around the room I saw cooperative learning and peer editing in English. They really wanted to get it right, and they took pleasure in e-mailing their comics to family and friends. Their pride of accomplishment was palpable—one shy student even suggested I gather the class's creations in a comic book and present it to the program director (which I did).

EXPANDING THE BOUNDARIES

This section comprises six chapters that open up a typical definition of multilevelness to include more kinds of diversity than simply linguistic. Chapter 11, "Culturally Responsive Teaching in a Colorful Classroom," by Roby Marlina, discusses how culturally responsive teaching, a concept typically associated with multicultural education, can be a pedagogically appropriate orientation within a multilevel language classroom. The discussion revolves around a practical classroom activity involving color associations and stereotypes.

Chapter 12, "Unity and Diversity in a Theology Class: Learning English for Academic Reading and Writing," by Iris Devadason, is set within the understudied context of seminary ESOL or theological English as a branch of English for specific purposes. Devadason presents a nuanced understanding of how "students training in theology in a mixed-ability English class in India need to work together from the start of their careers in order to foster a sense of oneness, participation, and peaceful cooperation" (p. 132–133).

Chapter 13, "Teaching *With* Students: Effective Instruction in Culturally and Linguistically Diverse Classrooms," by Karla Garjaka, explicitly expands the idea of multilevel classrooms to include multiple forms of cultural and linguistic diversity, which she regards not as barriers but as valuable resources. Garjaka, originally from Brazil and now working in a large midwestern U.S. city, includes numerous practical teaching tips that flesh out a model built on respect, comfort, understanding, and interaction.

Chapter 14, "Minds Working Together: Scaffolding Academic Writing in a Mixed-Ability EFL Class," by Le Van Canh and Nguyen Thi Thuy Minh, takes a sociocultural perspective on meeting the demands of academic writing in a foreign language: "If learning how to produce writing that satisfies academic norms is the problem from a student's perspective, from a teacher's perspective the challenge is to prepare students with varying English proficiencies and from non-English-speaking cultural and academic backgrounds to become flexible writers who can effectively tackle academic writing tasks from a variety of angles" (p. 150). The authors explore various forms of scaffolding and report on the most effective strategies.

Chapter 15, "Self-Access Language Learning: Accommodating Diversity," by Garold Murray, connects the literature on multilevel classrooms and self-access language learning, as seen concretely in one center established in a northern Japanese city. Conceptualizing the center as one form of a community of practice, Murray explains a philosophy and structure that enable and empower an incredibly multilevel and diverse group of learners.

Chapter 16, "Building a Community of Mixed-Ability Learners: Connect, Network, Empower," by Jo Bertrand, gives an inside perspective on two Chinese classrooms, one for nuclear engineers and one for secondary school English teachers. Faced with varying language proficiencies and professional statuses as well as a cross-cultural (teacher–student) learning situation, Bertrand developed an approach to task design that gave participants adequate help and freedom or space, guidance without domination, and confidence to work together to meet their language learning goals.

We are pleased to present this bundle of sticks to you as readers, and we are grateful to TESOL for allowing us and the contributors to add to the growing knowledge base of classroom practice in language education. We hope that this volume and the Classroom Practice Series as a whole will be an encouragement and help to you as you continue to create and collect your own bundles of sticks. Teachers who value professional development and diversity are indeed teachers who thrive in multilevel or mixed-ability classrooms and who understand the strength that flows from unity.

Bradley Baurain is currently a PhD student at the University of Nebraska–Lincoln, in the United States. He has taught ESOL and teacher education courses for more than 15 years in China, the United States, and Vietnam. He has presented widely and previously edited Teacher's Edition, *a journal in the field of TESOL focused on Southeast Asia. His research interests include moral, spiritual, and religious issues in teacher identity and practice; teacher education and development; and imaginative literature in language teaching and learning.*

Phan Le Ha is a faculty member at Monash University, in Australia, as well as a visiting lecturer at Vietnam National University and Hanoi Open University, in Vietnam. She has presented widely and is the author of Teaching English as an International Language: Identity, Resistance, and Negotiation *(Multilingual Matters, 2008). Her research interests include the relationships among language, culture, society, pedagogy, and identity; English as an international language; and academic writing across cultures.*

Standing Before a
Sea of Faces

CHAPTER 2

Responding to the Challenge of Large Mixed-Ability Classes in China

Alan Seaman

Several years ago, after teaching a graduate course in foreign language teaching methods in the United States, I read through the anonymous course evaluations to find this plaintive note:

> Progressive techniques for language teaching are fascinating, but I will probably go back to doing the same old thing when I return to China. I had 356 students in my classes last term. Typically, I have over 50 students in a class. There is no way I can adopt a new methodology, so I will stick with my usual approach: lectures and tests.

These comments presented me with a distinct challenge. Many of the graduate students in my classes—those from North America as well as other areas of the world—had been working as English language teachers in Asia. It was not enough to say to these students, "Here is the methodology; just try to make it work." But on the other hand, I could not in good conscience encourage them to rely on lectures as their primary approach. Although I had previously taught in China, my class sizes had never exceeded 25 students. How would it be possible to use methodology designed for an "ideal" class size within the context described in the course evaluation comment?

To add another layer of complexity, I realized that oversized classes inherently tend to include students from a variety of proficiency levels. The very size of these classes increases the likelihood that they will be mixed-ability groupings. My previous classes in China had been somewhat mixed-ability even when the programs had attempted to separate students into different levels for instruction. Increasingly, however, I was hearing about teachers who were assigned to teach broadly defined courses such as "Sophomore English," which lumped together students with widely ranging levels of proficiency. The general nature of these courses magnified the challenges associated with multilevel instruction.

CONTEXT

To deal with these issues directly, I recently served as a visiting professor at a major Chinese university during a 6-month sabbatical. Tianjin University, in the city of Tianjin, in northeastern China, is classified as a high-ranking "key university," with a particular focus on science and technology. When I was assigned to teach English to five classes of graduate students, in addition to providing a methodology course for English Department faculty, I responded with alacrity. Each of my five classes would have 60 students, for a total of 300 students in addition to the 40 Chinese English professors in my professional development class.

The size of these classes will not be surprising to teachers who have worked in China in recent years. The rapid growth of the university system, combined with rising demand for English language instruction, has often resulted in English language teachers being spread across as many students as possible. During the first 3 years of the 21st century, China's enrollments in higher education more than doubled (R. Hu, Chen, & Mao, 2004). Throughout the primary and secondary levels, class sizes of 50 or more are commonplace and accepted (Din, 1998). Din notes that some of the primary-level teachers she researched classified any class with under 50 students as "small."

I also learned that my classes would inevitably be mixed-ability due to the nature of graduate study. Many of the younger graduate students came directly from undergraduate programs that included quite a bit of English language instruction. The older students (those beyond the age of 30) were returning to academia after years of little or no English study. In general, these older students had a higher level of anxiety about the class and lower self-esteem about their English language abilities. The range of ages (approximately 23–42) guaranteed a complex, multilevel classroom. As Hess (2001) notes, language classes, especially large ones, are inherently heterogeneous in "genders, maturity, occupations, ethnicities, cultural and economic backgrounds, as well as personalities" (p. 2). Variation in age, in particular, would be a primary source of the multiple proficiency levels in my classes.

The physical nature of the classroom added to the challenge. Located in an older academic building on campus, the classroom featured rows of bolted-down desks and chairs, all facing the chalkboard and podium at the front of the room. A row of windows lined one side of the classroom. At the front of the room was a console with a personal computer that was connected to a data projector on the ceiling. This technology allowed me to project slides and videos in class, but it presented its own challenges. Frequent power outages, some lasting just a second, meant laboriously restarting the computer and finding the appropriate slide while continuing to teach the class. Because of this, I would have to be sparing in my use of the projector. Along with the large number of students, almost everything in the physical context pointed toward a lecture-and-test approach.

Although this situation was hardly ideal for language teaching, at least from my Western perspective, it presented me with an invaluable opportunity to mediate between current methodology and the realities of a large, mixed-ability classroom. I would also have the opportunity to teach a difficult schedule and simultaneously engage in dialogue with my Chinese colleagues about my ideas as they developed.

Over a period of 6 months, I developed a systematic approach that I hoped would be successful in raising the English proficiency level of my students and moving them further toward their professional goals for English. This approach had the following components:

1. defining my principles

2. surveying student interests and goals

3. creating a predictable lesson structure

4. organizing the class into work units

5. encouraging meaningful communication

6. using assessment to build proficiency

I created most of these components in response to pragmatic concerns and a busy schedule, which allowed little time for reflection. I did, however, discuss my methodological ideas each week with the group of Chinese English teachers in the professional development class that I was also teaching.

I was somewhat concerned that my Anglocentric knowledge base was being imposed on students in a different cultural context (Canagarajah, 1999, p. 210). Fortunately, the responses of my Chinese colleagues provided insights into how well my intuitions fit the local context. In the final section of this chapter, I engage in a sociocultural critique of my approach to this problem.

CURRICULUM, TASKS, MATERIALS

After receiving a description of my teaching assignment by e-mail from the department chair at Tianjin University, I spent some time considering how I would approach the teaching of five classes of 60 students each. I wanted to avoid taking the easy way out—simply developing a 2-hour lecture and repeating it across the five classes each week. As a bottom line, I wanted students to grow significantly in their communicative competence in English as a result of taking my course. As a starting point, I went through an exercise I frequently use before creating a new course: I (re)define my teaching philosophy and narrow it down to a set of nonnegotiable principles.

Step 1: Defining My Principles

As I brainstormed a set of principles, I realized that I wanted to preserve the following characteristics:

- development of communicative competence (i.e., the ability to use English for authentic communicative purposes) as a major goal

- an emphasis on collaboration and interaction

- an emphasis on authentic tasks

- an emphasis on individualizing and personalizing instruction, rather than teaching all students in the same way

- careful assessment of individual student performance

Most of these principles are commonplace assumptions about foreign language teaching in current methodology used in the United States—the sort of principles one finds in teacher training workshops and popular textbooks (e.g., H. D. Brown, 2007). They are all related to the larger construct of proficiency, which has been a hallmark of my teaching for a number of years as a result of the influence of Alice Omaggio-Hadley (1993). Essentially, I asked myself how I could construct a course that would enable students to move to a higher level of proficiency in the four skill domains of reading, writing, speaking, and listening.

Once these principles had been defined, I then asked myself a pragmatic question: How could I apply these ideas to 300 students in five classes without working myself to death or alienating the students?

Step 2: Surveying Student Interests and Goals

After meeting with the English Department chair to review the university's goals for the course, I developed a broad outline of topics and reading selections for the 16-week semester. As a foreign professor, I was given the topic of "American culture" as a focus for a course that would raise students' English language proficiency across the four skill domains. The MA and PhD students from various departments in my classes were also required to take courses in English language writing and speaking from Chinese English professors at the university. The department chair and dean assumed that the students would be interested in learning about U.S. culture from a native of the United States and that this interest would motivate them to attend my classes. This intrinsic motivation would hopefully keep them going in classes that would largely be taught monolingually, unlike the bilingual approach used by the Chinese professors.

Despite the department chair's optimism and belief in my ability to motivate the students, I knew from past experience that several potential problems lay ahead. Graduate students at this key university were unlikely to view a foreign professor as a novelty. Foreign English teachers have been working in China for more than two decades and can easily be viewed as normal or even by some as an annoyance. Moreover, in classes with enrollments of 60, it would be easy for students to miss class sessions unnoticed. I knew of foreign teachers starting out with 60 enthusiastic students in the first week and ending up with a core of 25 by the middle of the semester, with the full class finally reconvening for the final exam. In many programs with large class sizes, attrition is expected and may even be welcomed by busy students and beleaguered teachers.

To make my course more relevant to the students and more intrinsically motivating, I developed a questionnaire that I gave to all classes during the first week (see Appendix A). This 1-page questionnaire asked for basic demographic information and had students identify the most important areas of cultural content from an extensive list. It also asked them to rate the most important skill domains in terms of their own proficiency and in terms of their goals for the future. The questionnaire concluded with several open-ended items that allowed students to ask questions and identify areas of concern.

As I pored over the 300 surveys, coming up with simple frequency counts for most of the items, a general pattern emerged. Most of the students were in the hard or applied sciences—areas such as physics, chemistry, mechanical engineering, and computer science. This was consistent with the identity of the university. Few had an interest in cultural topics such as recreation or food; they were mostly interested in scientific and technical topics and in related areas such as business and education. In terms of English proficiency, they were concerned most about their perceived weaknesses in listening, speaking, and, to a lesser degree, writing. Most saw reading as their strongest skill.

The open-ended questions (and several follow-up conversations I had with students) indicated that few students planned to travel to the United States for tourism or study or to interact regularly with people from the United States. They needed higher proficiency in English so that they could communicate professionally with other nonnative speakers of English. This might mean traveling to Japan for a symposium that would be conducted in English or working with a multinational research team in China in which English would be the common lingua franca. A female chemical engineer, for instance, approached me at the end of the first class session to explain that she would be traveling to Germany for the next 2 weeks to meet with a German engineering firm, communicating mainly in English. Given these purposes, it seemed pointless to focus the course primarily on U.S. culture.

During the second week of the course, I returned to my classes with a dramatically revised syllabus. A number of general cultural topics had disappeared, and the focus had shifted to four areas (science, technology, business, and education) that were most relevant to the students' interests and goals. In addition, the course content had shifted away from American culture toward cross-cultural studies, with a new focus on anthropological categories that can be broadly used to understand and compare cultures: collectivism and individualism, universalism and particularism, monochronic and polychronic views of time, and direct and indirect forms of communication. I drew much of this material from books by Geert Hofstede (1997) and Craig Storti (1999). My hope was to shift the content focus to information that would help these students work cross-culturally with colleagues from countries ranging from Germany and Korea to Brazil and India, in addition to the United States and the United Kingdom.

Step 3: Creating a Predictable Lesson Structure

Once the focus of the course had been defined, the next task was to create a predictable lesson structure, a kind of operating system for the class. In large, mixed-ability classes, it is especially important to use a structured approach in order to minimize time spent giving instructions. Once students have been socialized into certain established routines, their energy can be directed to the content of particular lessons. I wanted to develop a pattern that could be repeated throughout the course.

My 2-hour lessons included a short break after the first hour and followed this pattern, which provided structure while allowing variety:

- quick introductory activity in groups or pairs

- listening practice and quiz

- illustrated lecture of content

- group discussion of content

- group task related to content

- follow-up discussion of task

- collecting group folders and giving the reading assignment for the next class

Each lesson was built around a particular theme, and the general movement of the class was from receptive skills (reading, listening) toward productive skills (speaking, writing).

Why did I choose this particular pattern? In the questionnaires, a majority of the students had emphasized listening and speaking as areas of needed growth. As a result, the heavy emphasis on listening skills in the first half of the lesson would be much appreciated. During the first half, students would build a common set of concepts and vocabulary that they could then put to use during the second half of the class, which involved task-based discussion and writing. I decided to build many of these tasks around the analysis of case studies or simulations involving the work of scientific researchers, engineers, and high-tech businesspeople (see the sample task in Appendix B).

The progression in this lesson structure was vitally important for older students with lower levels of English language proficiency. The general movement from receptive language (particularly via the illustrated lecture) toward productive language gave them time to prepare mentally for the more stressful tasks involving speaking. The second half of the lesson began with individual work that was intended to provide them with further scaffolding prior to speaking English with others in groups. Although they might not be able to speak as fluently as the younger students, they at least had something written down to add to the discussion.

Teachers in other contexts will choose different patterns based on the goals of their students. The general principle is to structure any large class with a clearly defined regular pattern.

Step 4: Organizing the Class Into Work Units

An obvious problem faced by teachers of large classes is the task of learning students' names and keeping track of attendance and assignments. I didn't want to waste time at the beginning of each class calling the 60 names on the roll, but I did want to encourage regular attendance and participation in the course. Because I am not particularly good at learning names, and my classes were far too large for typical name games such as a tossing a ball around, I had to develop a different approach.

My solution was based on the Chinese concept of *danwei,* or "work unit"—a basic social structure within modern Chinese society. Traditionally, most urban residents in China have belonged to a *danwei,* such as a factory or university, and this serves as an important basis of their social identification. I always carried my own identification card for my *danwei,* the university where I was employed, so I realized this would be a familiar concept to students.

I divided each class into 20 *danwei* groups of three students each, gave each group a number, and asked the students always to sit together. My class roll had students' names listed according to these groups. Once they were in these groups during a lesson, I could easily use the class roll to determine who was or was not present that day. This strategy also helped me learn students' names much more easily than if I were to gaze out at a large, amorphous jumble of faces in the classroom.

Borrowing an idea from Nancy Mutoh (1998), I gave each *danwei* group a manila folder that the group leader picked up at the beginning of each lesson. By collecting written assignments in these folders during each class, I could read through them in the same sequence of names that I had in my grade book. This made record keeping much easier than if I had collected a randomly arranged pile of papers each time I picked up assignments.

Step 5: Encouraging Meaningful Communication

My 1950s-era classroom had the traditional rows of desks, all bolted to the floor and facing the front. This type of classroom, still common throughout the world, is less than ideal for group work. If students were sitting during a group discussion, they had to twist their bodies around in awkward positions in order to face each other. My solution was simple: When I wanted students to have a small-group discussion in English, I often asked them to stand and face each other. Not only was this slight shift in format authentic—in real life we often talk to each other while standing—but it also led to a dramatic increase in energy level among the students.

Because it is unusual for older Chinese students in a large class to raise their hands and initiate questions, I also developed different strategies for the question-and-answer segments of the lesson. One strategy was to have students take 5 minutes to write down one or two questions that they had about the day's topic. This way, everyone had a question ready for the discussion, even students at lower proficiency levels. As I responded to their questions and asked follow-up questions, I gained a deeper understanding of what the students were thinking and found myself intrigued by their distinct perspectives on issues ranging from foreign policy to world trade to the promises and dangers of technology.

The very nature of the course encouraged communication through bicultural dialogue. After focusing on general categories for analyzing culture and hearing about one aspect of U.S. culture in the listening segment, students had their turn to write and speak. As they used the categories to analyze Chinese culture and compare it with that of the United States, they became my cultural informants.

Step 6: Using Assessment to Build Proficiency

Assessment can be daunting for teachers facing large classes. With 300 students, I was challenged to set up a final test or project that involved meaningful use of language but would also be fairly easy to score.

In the Chinese educational system, final exams are extremely important. To put this reality to good use, I wanted to make my final exam as authentic as possible so it would have a positive influence on the instruction leading up to the exam. Most of the students prepared carefully for the exam by attending lectures, taking listening quizzes, writing short papers, and participating orally in tasks involving analysis of cultural situations. In other words, the nature of the final exam encouraged students to attend class regularly and participate in communicative activities.

The exam was structured in three segments. The first was a listening section that involved an original lecture I had recorded myself, during which students could take notes. They used these notes to answer 20 questions about the content of the lecture. The second segment was a multiple-choice survey of the content of the course. The final section involved writing two short essays in response to scenarios similar to the ones we had analyzed in class.

I was especially pleased with the high level of critical thinking expressed in English on the essay section of the exam. As students responded analytically to the real-world scenarios, they often surprised me with their clear, forceful prose. By analyzing situations involving scientists, engineers, and economists, the students gained a useful conceptual framework that they could apply to their work in the future involving people from a variety of cultures and in a variety of professional contexts.

REFLECTIONS

By the end of the course, I was satisfied that most of the students had made progress toward higher levels of proficiency in the four skill domains—particularly speaking and listening—and had gained an ability to use anthropological categories for cultural analysis. The systematic use of the *danwei* work units had encouraged a high level of class attendance, and students were focused both on real-world goals for their use of English in scientific or business contexts across a range of cultures and on preparing for the final examination. My sense that the course was successful was reinforced by the unsolicited comments of several students. One older doctoral student, near the end of the course, said (in a typically analytical fashion), "At the beginning I understood about 25% of what you were saying, and now I understand 75%!"

Could I trust my intuitions about the success of this course? To answer this question, I needed one final step to add to the previous six. This step involved critically examining my assumptions about language learning (formulated largely in the United States) in light of the Chinese context in which I was working. In this context, the application of critical pedagogy was as important as my initial brainstorming of the principles that guided my teaching. To guide this reflection, I draw on two resources that I have found to be particularly cogent: Suresh Canagarajah's (1999) discussion of critical pedagogy in *Resisting Linguistic Imperialism in English Teaching* and Adrian Holliday's (2005) discussion of foreign teachers in *The Struggle to Teach English as an International Language*.

Canagarajah (1999) makes a distinction between the "pedagogy of the mainstream" and "critical pedagogy" (p. 16). From this perspective, my nonnegotiable principles in Step 1 were clearly in the category of mainstream pedagogy. They were derived from my training and experience in a particular cultural context (the United States) and were in line with the dominant pedagogy of communicative language teaching. Citing the influence of Claire Kramsch, Canagarajah notes that "communicative pedagogy inducts students into the foreign culture in a non-reflexive manner, often insensitive to the ideological implications of this induction" (p. 188). Adherents of critical pedagogy would argue that my emphasis on communicative activities (and perhaps my entire approach to this situation) was grounded in a particular ideology that I was imposing on my students.

Although he is not writing specifically from the vantage point of critical pedagogy, Holliday (2005) also causes teachers to engage in reflection by problematizing many pedagogical characteristics or received truths that Western-educated teachers take for granted. For instance, he views such hallmarks of communicative teaching as the four skills, learner-centeredness, authenticity, and group work as cultural icons that have arisen in the West (p. 42). The danger is that they may be imposed on non-Western students and teachers in a way that perpetuates "native-speakerism" (p. 157), reinforcing the economic and political hegemony of the dominant English-speaking cultures.

Both Holliday and Canagarajah share similar concerns about the role and influence of Western teachers in non-Western contexts, although they express these concerns in distinct ways. Holliday (2005) focuses on teachers who "come from the English-speaking West and are characterized by having an overactive professional zeal connected with the notion that English and English teaching is originally theirs" (p. 3). Writing from a different cultural vantage point, Canagarajah (2005) maintains that "we acknowledge the localness of each of our own knowledge that we have the proper humility to engage productively with other knowledge traditions. The assumption that one's knowledge is of sole universal relevance does not encourage conversation" (p. 20). Both argue that teachers from the West need to be aware of how their knowledge has been constructed and avoid using this knowledge in ways that perpetuate Western hegemony. Both are optimistic that this is possible in the classroom. For instance, on a practical level, Canagarajah (1999) argues that foreign English teachers "have the ethical responsibility of negotiating the hidden values and interests behind knowledge, and are expected to help students adopt a critical orientation in learning" (p. 17).

How can a teacher overwhelmed with the task of teaching large classes possibly apply the tenets of critical pedagogy? Looking back at my six-step approach, I can identify several instances that directly or indirectly began to help my students adopt a critical orientation in learning. For example, by using a questionnaire to gather information from students and then adjusting the syllabus to focus on topics and skills they had identified as important, I was granting them a certain level of power to determine the content of the course. This resulted in a second important application of critical pedagogy—the shift away from an exclusive focus on U.S. culture toward a discussion of categories that could be used to examine critically both U.S. and Chinese cultures. This shift set up a cultural dialectic in my classrooms that echoed Canagarajah's (1999) suggestion to "let students negotiate the borders of each culture as they confront the foreign language" (p. 188) instead of focusing on either Western culture or students' native cultures. My emphasis on critical appraisal of cultures also moved the discussion away from a danger that Holliday (2005) calls *culturism*—a reductionist, stereotypical, essentialist approach to describing the cultures of others.

Upon reflection, I can also locate features of my approach that privileged local knowledge and encouraged critical reflection. By adopting the *danwei* groups as a management strategy, I was appropriating a familiar concept from the Chinese context rather than imposing a strategy from outside. Similarly, my emphasis on the final examination reinforced an important aspect of Chinese university life instead of replacing it with Western-style projects or activities. Finally, by linking so many of the class activities to preparation for the final exam and to professional goals identified by the students, these activities became infused with a more serious purpose.

As He (2005) notes, looking back at her experiences during two decades of teaching in China, Chinese students often responded negatively to communicative activities that "did not constitute any serious learning in a Chinese sense" (p. 19). At the same time, she says that "with China's entry into the WTO [World Trade Organization], English is no longer simply a subject in the school curriculum, but an instrument for work and daily communication" (p. 14). This tension between a suspicion of communicative methodology and a desire to prepare students for communication in a global society is also a significant theme in English teachers' essays compiled by Parry and Su (1998). In my classroom, communicative activities were not simply games; they were linked both to the final exam and to students' real-world goals for the use of English.

Perhaps most important, through these tasks I emphasized communication in English as an international language (EIL) as opposed to employing the English and culture of the United States as the targets. My students focused on contexts where English is a medium of communication with colleagues who, like them, had studied it as an additional language. Philosophically, this is in line with Widdowson's powerful claim that

> how English develops in the world is no business whatever of the native speakers in England, the United States, or anywhere else. . . . The very fact that English is an international language means that no nation can have custody over it. . . . It is not a possession which they lease out to others, while still retaining the freehold. (quoted in Holliday, 2005, p. 8)

Widdowson's conceptualization of EIL reinforces the common Chinese view of English as an instrument or tool that is useful in the country's broader program of modernization rather than a means of acquiring U.S. or British culture (He, 2005, p. 12). My Chinese students and colleagues desired to learn English on their own terms. As a result, I was less interested in the students meeting a U.S. standard for pronunciation, grammar, or language functions than in expanding the breadth of what they could do with English in their professional lives. The goal was fluency and intelligibility, not "native-speaker-like" English according to a U.S. or British standard.

In facing the difficulties of the context—the large class sizes, the range of proficiencies, the physical limitations of the classrooms—I would have done students a disfavor by falling back on a lecture-and-test format or by forcing them into a series of communicative activities focusing on U.S. English and culture as the learning targets. What they needed most was a context where they could engage in critical reflection and at the same time grow in English language proficiency. Looking back on this experience and discussing it with my current graduate students, I take comfort in Holliday's (2005) acknowledgment that "educators and students from outside the English-speaking West have immense abilities to make English and TESOL what they wish them to be" (p. 11). I realize now that facing the "problem" of teaching large, mixed-ability classes forced me out of my habitual approach to teaching English and stimulated me to find solutions that were more sensitive to students' cultural context.

Alan Seaman is an associate professor and director of the MA TESOL program at Wheaton College, in Illinois, in the United States. He teaches courses in applied linguistics and has presented workshops for teachers in more than 15 countries. He was also an active member of the National Editorial Council for the English: No Problem! *course book series from New Readers Press.*

APPENDIX A: STUDENT QUESTIONNAIRE

English as a Foreign Language for Doctoral Students

STUDENT INFORMATION FORM

Please take a few minutes to fill out this form so the professor can get to know you as we begin this course.

Name: _____

Address: _____

E-mail address: _____

Graduate program: _____
          (What area are you studying for your degree?)

Years of English study: _____
          (How many years have you studied English?)

Have you had an American/British/Canadian/Australian
teacher before? _____

Please rate your proficiency in English in the following areas:

Skill Area	Weaker				Stronger
Reading	1	2	3	4	5
Writing	1	2	3	4	5
Speaking	1	2	3	4	5
Listening	1	2	3	4	5

What areas of American culture do you most want to learn about? (Check three areas and number them 1, 2, 3.)

___ history   ___ economy

___ businesses   ___ government

___ education   ___ media/journalism

___ urbanization (cities)   ___ science and technology

___ male-female relations   ___ older/younger generations

___ ethnic diversity   ___ entertainment

___ recreation/sports   ___ how Americans communicate

___ what Americans believe

What other areas would you like to learn about that are not listed above? List 2–5 more areas if you wish:

What questions do you have as we begin this course? Write 1–3 questions for the professor.

APPENDIX B: SAMPLE TASK

The Aruna Chemical Company has a factory with about 500 workers. This branch of the company makes materials for large ships.

One Monday morning, the president of the company asked the top engineers to come to an important meeting at 9:00. As the meeting began, several of the engineers arrived with cups of coffee and sweet rolls. During the meeting they finished eating their breakfast.

The president began by saying that one of the top engineers, Mr. Lee, had invented an exciting new plastic material that was very strong in seawater. The company president asked Mr. Lee to explain the chemical properties of the new plastic. Mr. Lee talked about the new plastic material for around 10 minutes. Then several engineers asked him follow-up questions about the material. One engineer (a woman) argued that an older form of plastic was better for ships. "Your plastic is too expensive for us to produce," she stated.

"I disagree completely," replied Mr. Lee. He explained that both plastics had already been compared in the laboratory and that the new one was much better.

The president announced that Mr. Lee would lead a team of engineers to develop cheaper ways to make the new plastic. Three engineers raised their hands and asked to be placed on the team. The president said that he hoped the material would receive a patent soon. Looking at his watch, he said, "Well, it's almost 9:45. We'd better be going."

How would you interpret this meeting culturally? Analyze the situation using the categories for cultural analysis we have discussed in class.

CHAPTER 3

Large Classes and Group Projects: A Curriculum Unit on Tourism in the Philippines

Doris H. Christopher and Roland A. Niez

Active learning is not only possible in large, multilevel classes, it is more engaging than instruction that is exclusively delivery or lecture style. Active learning (Harmin & Toth, 2006) produces better motivation and greater student involvement. This chapter presents one way of inspiring active learning in multilevel classes, focusing on a curriculum unit centered around promoting Biliran Island as a tourist destination in the Philippines. Student work is documented and discussed, including promotional brochures, tour guide role-plays, radio and television advertisements, and informational presentations about the various cultural groups on Biliran. Despite the challenges facing those of us who teach large, mixed-ability classes, this chapter demonstrates that we do not have to settle for less.

CONTEXT

Classes at the Naval Institute of Technology (Naval, pronounced *naVAAL*, is a city, not a reference to the U.S. military) are typically large, and tuition fees are low. This enables students from diverse backgrounds to apply and attend. Students in public schools in the Philippines attend 10 years of compulsory education—6 at the elementary level and 4 at the secondary level. Because there is no formal kindergarten, Filipino students begin first grade at age 7 or 8 and complete high school at age 17 or 18.

Language Backgrounds

Children on the island of Biliran in the Eastern Visayas grow up speaking either Cebuano or Waray at home; these languages are not mutually intelligible. The Naval Institute of Technology (NIT) also draws students from many areas of the

Biliran

AGTA BEACH RESORT, ALMERIA, BILIRAN

HIGATANGAN ISLAND

From the gallery of student work

Philippines where other languages are spoken, including Hiligaynon, also known as Ilonggo, in the Western Visayas and Ilokano; Tagalog; Kapampangan; and Chavakano (see Figure 1). Although students speak various languages at home, English is the only medium of instruction in the school system. Thus, students have experienced academic instruction in English prior to entering NIT. However, there is a wide variation in English proficiency levels, especially in speaking and listening. English may not have been used in the home, or high school instruction may have been more focused on reading and writing. The curriculum unit that is the subject of this chapter was taught to education students majoring in English. Courses for English majors at NIT combine English with literature and language arts.

Multilevel Students

Some students complete their secondary studies at the NIT Laboratory High School (LHS), where academic expectations are high and students achieve high levels of proficiency in English. LHS graduates are integrated into general NIT classes, leading automatically to mixed-ability classes because other students

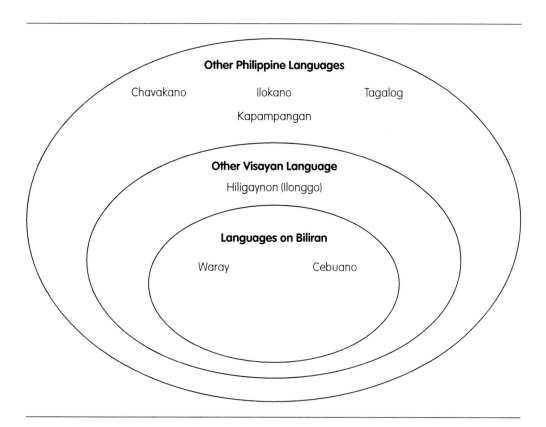

Figure 1. Biliran Languages in Relation to Other Philippine Languages at Naval Institute of Technology

Discover BILIRAN

As the new Millennium dawns, discover the Ageless beauty of Our Province, marvel her mysteries, experience nature at its very best... landscapes where the Creator is the artist Himself, and feel the warm hospitality we are known for.

A paradise waiting to be discovered not just by the world but by our own people as well.

Now enjoy them through BTC's affordable tour packages for all those dying to see the beauty of the islands.

From the gallery of student work

entering NIT are not as well prepared in English. Cooperative learning principles (Johnson, Johnson, & Holubec, 2002) suggest that groups be heterogeneous, and mixing ability levels is one way to achieve this. Heterogeneous groups generate more elaborative thinking, which increases depth of understanding and increases the breadth and quality of reasoning. These factors increase the likelihood of accurate, long-term retention of language learned (Johnson et al., 2002). Students in multilevel groups who have learned how to function effectively can generate more enthusiasm for their work while drawing on individual expertise in content and language.

In the curriculum reported on here, the teacher usually split the class of 35 students into seven groups. At least one of the accelerated learners (LHS graduates) was placed in each group. This structure better enabled everyone to understand the activity or task, provided for more equal participation, ensured that all students knew how to proceed, and helped everyone keep pace with the learning goals.

CURRICULUM, TASKS, MATERIALS

The curriculum unit—Promoting Biliran Island as a Tourist Destination in the Philippines—was inherently interesting to students, who spent a total of 3 hours per week in their English class. Each lesson extended for two or three class periods; the complete unit took about 8 weeks. In preparing the unit, major projects and tasks were initially determined based on content (tourism), then target language skills were identified, and finally specific lessons and activities were created. In this way, the planning process was consistent with the concept of backward design (McTighe & Wiggins, 2004).

Much of the unit focused on student-produced projects, including a promotional brochure, tour guide role-plays, and presentations of student-produced radio and television advertisements (see the Appendix for samples of student work). Another key project involved students representing their individual cultural groups by completing community-based research about music, language, major cultural events, food, beliefs, and practices, and giving oral presentations on these topics to their peers. Higher order thinking skills such as analysis, synthesis, and evaluation were necessary to complete these projects and tasks, using creativity and multiple literacies. In addition, selected language skills were reviewed or retaught.

Building Background

The theme of tourism called for specific information about Biliran. Facts about local tourism were provided via two documentaries from which students learned about the island's existing tourist industry. The videos provided two additional benefits. First, the class analyzed them to discover and articulate the dos and don'ts of oral presentations and public speaking. Second, using the videos

Travel/Accommodation Advisory

Name of Lodge/Inn	Type of Accommodation	Daily Rate (Php)
Rosevie Pension House Vicentillo St., Naval, Biliran Tel. No. 500-1377	Single (aircon) Single (non-aircon) Double (aircon, separate CR) Double (aircon, w/ CR) Meals upon request	300.00 250.00 400.00 500.00
Brigida Inn Castin St., Naval, Biliran Tel. No. 500-1379	Single (aircon) Single (non-aircon) Double (aircon) Double (non-aircon) Conference Room	450.00 70.00 500.00 90.00 100.00/hr
Marvin's Place Brgy. Atipolo, Naval, Biliran	Single (aircon) Whole place (room w/aircon, CR, Conference Room) Meals served upon request	600.00 600.00
Mondido Beach Resort San Agustin, Caibiran, Biliran	Room (non-aircon) Cottage	500.00 350.00/150.00

How to get there

Naval - Tacloban City and Naval - Ormoc City routes are served by economy buses and aircon Mega Taxis. Daily flights from Manila arrive at Tacloban City Airport, while Ormoc City is only 2 hours away by fast crafts from Cebu City.

CONTACT TEL. NO. 09128918931

From the gallery of student work

incorporated modern technology, which tended to heighten student motivation and enthusiasm (Shrum & Glisan, 2005). Although a lecture on tourist spots around Biliran would have given the same information, it would not have been as interesting to students. Further background was provided using an existing brochure titled "Fast Facts About Biliran," featuring history and other factual information about the island.

The documentaries and the brochure were authentic materials, that is, texts not specifically produced for second language learners. Such materials can be effective when teachers modify tasks to ensure student success in using them (Shrum & Glisan, 2005).

Additional background information was provided by means of a class field trip. Students went on a daylong bus tour of multiple tourist spots on Biliran, during which they were required to take notes on the facilities, resources, amenities, and history of each place; caretaker information; the number of tourists normally present; the ticket or entrance fee; and any general observations. After the field trip, they wrote reaction papers about their tour, which were graded half on effective expression and content accuracy and half on grammar. This assignment was begun in class, with the teacher reviewing first drafts and suggesting improvements.

Working on Language

To increase the potential success of this class on tourism, language components specific to the content were identified (Curtain & Dahlberg, 2004). In this unit, students became familiar with a map of Biliran Province, which provided a context for reviewing direction-related vocabulary, such as *north, south, east,* and *west.* Audiotapes giving directions on how to access various tourist spots provided related listening practice. Another language focus included greetings and appropriate introductions when interacting with tourists. Students practiced these in small groups, including different styles of greeting used in different cultures.

To create convincing and appealing tourist brochures, increasing students' facility with vocabulary, particularly adjectives, proved important and also gave a specific purpose to learning and reviewing certain grammar points (Shrum & Glisan, 2005). The "Fast Facts" brochure provided a good model for students in using adjectives. To accommodate the multilevel nature of the classes, teachers first had students report what they knew or could recall about adjectives and then elicited adjective definitions and categories from the class. Lastly, selected adjectives were presented and explained directly for lower level students. For homework, students watched the movie *Shrek* (Adamson & Jenson, 2001) and used descriptive adjectives to write an essay about the scenery and settings of the movie. This writing helped students paint vivid pictures with words in preparation for creating brochures that would be enticing for tourists.

Practice with question formation, using both *wh-* and yes/no questions, was necessary for the tour guide role-play activity. The role-play scenarios were meant to provide purposeful practice with these question types. To provide

From the gallery of student work

variety, scenarios involving crime were selected as fruitful topics that would engage students' interest while helping them practice question formation. In one assignment, students worked in pairs and played the role of either a witness to a kidnapping or a detective gathering information. For this particular task, they were allowed to use their home language to create the questions, which they then translated into English. By thinking and creating the questions first in their native language, students were able to produce more complex questions. A second scenario required them to assume the role of either a witness to a murder or a lawyer. Students wrote yes/no questions about the scenario and then role-played the situation within a small group. In general, the language activities focused on those aspects of language that were needed to communicate the content. Thus, the language components had a high degree of relevancy (Echevarria, Vogt, & Short, 2004), building interest and purpose.

Mastering Content in Small Groups

The content taught in this class touched on various topics, including general facts about Biliran, the locations and unique aspects of tourist spots, and information about cultural groups and practices on the island. Much of the content learning was not accomplished through lecture but rather via group work. In one group activity, students drew large maps of Biliran Province and labeled the various tourist sites, towns, and municipalities. Every student in a group was required to contribute to the map in some way—the joint creation of a single product is an example of positive goal interdependence (Johnson et al., 2002). By assigning each person in a group an individual role or task, the teacher encouraged all group members to participate in ways that matched their level of language proficiency. One person ensured that all locations on the map were correctly positioned. Another monitored participation so that each group member placed at least one tourist spot or town on the map. Another coordinated materials while others assisted with organizing the group or monitoring the speaking contributions of group members. These roles exemplify cooperative skills, which can be overtly taught to create well-functioning and productive groups. The four types of group work skills—forming, functioning, formulating, and fermenting (Johnson et al., 2002)—become progressively more complex and help to engage students of varying levels in a mixed-ability class.

Students may be randomly assigned to groups, or teachers may designate specific group membership. We feel that heterogeneous groups are best. In the map activity, high and low achievers were combined in every group. Separating disruptive personalities or incorporating isolated students may be other factors to consider when creating groups. Allowing students to select their own groups is recommended the least (Johnson et al., 2002) because the resulting groups tend to be more homogeneous and are often less likely to be on task. However, because students prefer to be with their friends, a compromise might be in order—they can be asked to list three people with whom they want to work, then at least one person from each student's list could be placed into his or her group. Lists might also prove helpful because they allow teachers to identify isolated students. A group of peers can then be built to support the isolated student (Johnson et al., 2002).

The groups formed for this curriculum unit were of various sizes, ranging from two to seven students each. It is more likely that all students become involved in the task when group size is small; students are less likely to "hide" or depend on other members to complete the task. However, other factors must sometimes be considered, and large groups can also be effective in certain situations or for certain objectives. Multiple and varied interactions are more possible in a larger group, but cooperative and interpersonal skills are necessary for proper group functioning. In a larger group, more resources and expertise are also collectively present, but more time is needed for activities. If the time allotted for a lesson is short, it is best to keep the group small (Johnson et al., 2002).

Preparing and Producing Brochures

Students were also required to do Internet research to find additional information about Biliran's tourist destinations. One particularly helpful feature of NIT is the availability of an Internet café on campus, which makes it possible for teachers to require computer-based assignments. To ensure that students have access, they can be allocated scheduled time outside of class hours. In their Internet research, students were required to identify major island industries and various tourist spots and attractions, learn more about the history of the province, and locate additional significant facts and information.

With all the information they had gathered, students prepared to make their own tourist brochures. In pairs, they exchanged opinions about their favorite locations on Biliran, an activity that required them to explain what they knew, share what they had learned, give an opinion, and provide reasons for their opinion. Each pair then shared their insights with another pair, creating groups of four and facilitating efficient feedback and debriefing.

To prepare for the written brochure, each student drew a picture of his or her favorite Biliran tourist attraction and wrote a descriptive paragraph rich in appropriate adjectives. It is important to note that there was a high degree of student choice in this activity, which is one way to provide an enriched, interesting, and motivating learning environment (Jensen, 2005). After drawing a picture, students produced first drafts of their brochures and received teacher feedback based on the rubric in Figure 2.

As students worked on their maps, drawings, and brochures, they gave each other feedback and provided peer critique on their efforts and products. They were also allowed to seek assistance from and interact with members of other groups. Such interaction and movement within the classroom is important because it strengthens the learning process, improves memory and information

Category	Slightly Meets Goals (0–2 points)	Moderately Meets Goals (3–5 points)	Mostly Meets Goals (6–8 points)	Entirely Meets Goals (9–10 points)
Design	Uses black and white only for the graphics, texts, and other content information	Uses a color other than black and white for the graphics, texts, and other content information	Applies several colors to emphasize the graphics, texts, and other content information	Contains all necessary colors for a glossy and attractive appearance of graphics, texts, and other content information
Content (e.g., places to visit, where to stay, how to get there, fast facts)	Very incomplete information	Little information	Adequate information	Complete information
Number of Tourist Spots and Pictures	No pictures and just one tourist spot	One or two pictures and two or three tourist spots	Three or four pictures and three or four tourist spots	All tourist spots and their corresponding pictures highlighted
Language and Grammar	All words, phrases, or expressions unclear or incorrectly written	Three words, phrases, or expressions unclear or incorrectly written	One or two words, phrases, or expressions unclear or incorrectly written	All words, phrases, and expressions clear and correctly written

Figure 2. Assessment Rubric for the Travel Brochure

retrieval, and increases student motivation (Jensen, 2005). Students clearly enjoyed learning actively during this phase of the unit.

Several factors contributed to the success of this assignment. First, students were able to complete the task because the lessons were segmented into small, manageable steps. Second, students saw the task of producing their own tourist brochures as one that was directly applicable to the real world, rather than as an academic abstraction (Echevarria et al., 2004). Third, students worked in stages, creating drafts that received specific feedback from the instructor. Feedback is one of the greatest sources of intrinsic motivation (Jensen, 2005). Fourth, students were given ample time to complete the project. Fifth, by receiving the rubric beforehand, students could understand more precisely the expectations and standards for the project. This knowledge motivated them to produce higher quality products. Finally, students developed and demonstrated their strengths in multiple literacies. As they drew, prepared maps, wrote text for brochures, did

PONDOL FALLS

SAMBAOAN ISLAND

From the gallery of student work

Internet research, and engaged in graphic design work, they experienced numerous multimodal language learning opportunities.

Role-Playing Tour Guides

The student work on question formation, as described earlier, provided the language preparation and practice for the tour guide role-play assignment. Pairs presented their role-plays in front of the class and were rated in four categories: voice quality and clarity, manner of delivery and fluency, use of bodily gestures, and facial expressions. To involve everyone and spur higher attention levels, students were told in advance that they would be called on randomly to give either positive feedback or constructive criticism about the presenting pair. Student comments from the audience were also graded.

Researching Communities

Student groups were assigned to research different local communities because tourists might want to learn about the cultures and customs of Biliran. They visited their assigned community on one weekend day for two consecutive weekends. They were required to investigate the songs, dances, crafts, and cultural products produced locally within their assigned community. Personal interviews with residents further revealed the uniqueness of each culture. Each group member was required to keep a journal or notebook of his or her findings, then group members combined the results of their individual research. Investigating the various cultures had more than an informational function; it also helped students become more aware of their own heritage as well as of the cultures of others.

After students completed their research, groups were required to report on how they had obtained their information. They presented their results as skits, performing dances, songs, and dramatic stories distinct to their particular community. Groups were given time to rehearse and practice, and appropriate cultural attire made the presentations colorful and authentic.

Several NIT teachers acted as judges and selected the top performing group. Grading criteria included accurate presentation of customs, attire and appearance, overall presence and appeal, stage deportment, and accuracy of the subject being portrayed. Students were also graded individually by the instructor. After their presentations, they were questioned by means of a written quiz to determine their level of involvement in both the research and the performance. Final marks were based on individual quiz and group performance grades, which provided students with opportunities to demonstrate what they had learned to the best of their ability and level.

Producing Radio and Television Commercials

In the final project for this curriculum unit, students worked in groups to write radio advertisements and television commercial scripts promoting Biliran as a tourist destination. Presentation of these advertisements and scripts reinforced and improved their oral English skills and increased their self-confidence in using the language. Students rehearsed and practiced before presenting their material. These presentations were evaluated based on comprehensiveness, appeal, grammar, language use, and overall flow.

More on Group Work in Large Classes

Large classes can be easily divided for pair and group work. In a classroom whose desks are arranged in rows and columns, pairs may be formed by having columns turn to face one another. Students may sit or stand in this pairing. To convert pairs into groups of four, the pair in front turns to face the pair behind. New pairs can be formed with only minimal movement: The first column stays seated, each student in the next column moves up one seat, and the person in front takes the back seat. This type of pair changing is useful for brief discussions, practice with dialogues, and reviewing.

Here is a technique that works well for oral review of material, such as vocabulary items. Have everyone in a chosen column stand up. Ask each student a question; if he or she answers it correctly, the student can sit down. When only one person remains standing, the corresponding row that includes that student must stand up, and the activity proceeds. Continue in this way until a large number of students have stood and answered questions. Everyone remains engaged as students listen to their classmates and watch to see if their row or column might be next.

REFLECTIONS

This integrated unit wove content and skills together with the theme of tourism. Students learned content as they prepared for their projects and presentations, which provided a purpose for the language components they practiced. The projects had clear goals and purposes. Students saw practical applications for their work in the unit.

Projects and class activities required all students to become involved, regardless of level, but with an openness guaranteeing that students of all levels could participate meaningfully. By combining students of various levels into groups, the teacher encouraged everyone to work together and contribute in order to complete the projects and activities. Grades were often given for pairs or groups, but also for individuals. Projects and activities were part of the grading process, but so were more traditional paper-and-pencil tests. Therefore, mixed-ability groupings of students had significant opportunities not only to assist one another but also to demonstrate their own proficiency and achievement.

Although expectations and standards were high, this curriculum unit was quite motivating for students. Projects were hands-on, and individual choice within project guidelines increased student engagement and allowed individual skills and expertise to shine. In addition to personal choice, other factors that motivated students included the variety of tasks and activities, the need to be an active listener or performer in order to contribute to pair and group work, the opportunity to work in groups, and the validation of students' cultures.

The materials that students created also incorporated and practiced a variety of skills. Interpersonal skills were required and refined as students worked in groups. Computer skills were developed as students searched the Internet for historical and tourist information on Biliran. Ethnographic and action research skills came into play when students traveled to diverse communities and conducted interviews on cultural perspectives and practices. They also practiced providing and accepting peer feedback and enhanced their presentation skills. Regardless of students' language levels, the teacher led all students to grow both academically and socially by requiring active participation that called on their cognitive, interpersonal, and presentation skills.

Doris H. Christopher works in preservice teacher education and graduate programs at the University of Hawaii, in the United States. She has taught in Saudi Arabia, Iran, and the Dominican Republic, as well as in public schools in the United States.

Roland A. Niez teaches at the Naval Institute of Technology, in Biliran, in the Philippines. As a Ford Foundation Scholar, he has completed graduate coursework in curriculum studies at the University of Hawaii.

CHAPTER 4

Speaking in Crowds: Oral Activities for Large Classes With Few Resources

Susan Donnelly Renaud, Elizabeth Tannenbaum, and Michael Jerald

The ideas presented in this chapter, which deal with developing and teaching effective speaking lessons for students in crowded classrooms, had their genesis in our collective teaching and teacher training experiences in several developing countries in the Middle East, Asia, Central America, and Africa over a span of more than 30 years. We taught classes that often had no more than a rough board painted black and soft, messy chalk for resources. The schools did not have photocopy machines, few of the students could afford textbooks, and they had to supply their own paper.

We began working together in Haiti in 2002. For five consecutive summers, we conducted a 4-week intensive certificate program in teaching English to speakers of other languages (TESOL) for Haitian English teachers from around the country and preservice teachers from the State Teacher Training College, in Port au Prince. At first, coming from the privileged environment of Canada and the United States and in spite of our previous teaching experiences, we did not fully grasp the realities of teaching English, or any subject, in Haiti. In many countries, Haiti included, teachers are poorly trained and have few resources with which to work. Classes can have 60–100 students meeting in rooms built for half those numbers. We soon realized that our certificate trainees could not possibly apply much of what we were presenting to them. Many of our student-centered techniques for fostering communication in the classroom seemed irrelevant, even laughable, yet we had teachers who wanted to teach effectively, and they had students who wanted to learn.

This, then, was our challenge—to share with Haitian English teachers an approach to teaching spoken language with activities that would work in their specific contexts. During our time in Haiti, we received advice from teachers who were experiencing these on-the-ground realities, and we benefited greatly from what we learned from them, including research they had conducted (especially Edouard, 2006; Pierre, 2005). In this chapter, we present the results of our work in a way that we hope will be of use to ESOL teachers in similar situations.

We began with a couple of seemingly simple questions: What is a successful speaking activity? What was the goal at which we would be aiming? Based on our own experience and input from sources such as Ur (1996) and Thornbury (2003), we settled on the following five ideas that should characterize successful activities:

1. *Learners talk quite a bit:* The activity should generate a great deal of speaking, using a wide variety of language. Learners must spend most of the time devoted to an activity actually engaged in conversation (e.g., exchanging information, negotiating meaning, coming to an agreement, solving a problem).

2. *Participation is even:* The activity should be organized in such a way that all members of a group must speak, not just the talkative or assertive ones. There should be equal opportunity for everyone to contribute and interact.

3. *Motivation is high:* The topic or task must be interesting and challenging to students. They must have something they want to say about it and be eager to achieve the objective of the task.

4. *Language is at an appropriate level:* Learners should have the language necessary to accomplish the task, in terms of both structure and vocabulary. The activity should oblige learners to use language they possess, but push them to the limits of their language ability.

5. *The objective of the activity is clear to learners:* They should experience some kind of closure at the end of the activity, which lets them know that they have successfully accomplished the task.

CONTEXT

According to a study cited by Ur (1996), the average perception of a "large" class is around 50 students, but she suggests that "the exact number does not really matter: what matters is how you, the teacher, see the class size in your own specific situation" (p. 302). Baker and Westrup (2000) echo this thought: "A large class can be any number of students, if the teacher feels there are too many students for them all to make progress" (p. 2). "Largeness" of a class is relative to the size of a room, the teacher's interpersonal and management skills, and the nature of the activities. In Haiti, we have observed and taught classes of up to 80 students in which communicative activities were used successfully.

In this chapter, we address only activities that allow students free use and practice of language that they learned previously. It goes without saying that these activities must be scaffolded and students prepared for the tasks in order for them to be successful.

What are the challenges of using oral activities in large classes, and how can teachers deal with these challenges? The following are some of the challenges that the Haitian teachers brought to our attention when we asked them why they had problems using communicative methods in their classes. In response to these challenges, we suggest some possible solutions.

Classroom Management

Challenge: When the teacher tries to organize group or pair work, the class gets out of control and students don't participate. One solution is to create an atmosphere of cooperation by involving students in setting classroom rules and norms of behavior. At the beginning of the year, ask them to work in small groups to write down rules that they think are reasonable for classroom behavior and the consequences for breaking those rules. If the rules come from students, who consider them to be fair, the students will be more willing to follow them.

Challenge: During group- or pair-work activities, students make too much noise and teachers in the other classrooms complain. One response is to make students aware of the problem and to explain that they do not need to speak loudly in order to be heard by the person next to them. If they understand that the alternative to speaking more quietly is listening to the teacher lecture, they will likely cooperate. Another idea is to set up signals for silence—using hand signals, a bell, a light, or some other approach. Often students themselves can help maintain discipline, such as when one student in each group is given the role of rule keeper. It might also be worth discussing with students the importance of showing respect for others by listening. Not every activity needs to be done at maximum volume!

Challenge: When students are asked to form groups, they often take too much time and are noisy when moving around. By the time they are ready, there is not enough time to do the activity. In this case, it might be advisable to establish routines and set the same groups and partners for a certain period of time. Another idea is to ask students to turn around and work with those in the row behind them, which eliminates the need to stand, walk around, and move desks and chairs (for additional ideas, see chapter 3 in this volume).

Challenge: Students make many mistakes when speaking English. If they work in groups, they hear low-quality input and continue to make the same errors. Research has shown that this is not necessarily true. According to R. Ellis (1986), for example, the negotiation of meaning—when learners interact with other learners and strive for mutual understanding—contributes to language acquisition in a number of ways, such as encouraging scaffolded instruction through peer interactions.

Challenge: Some students refuse to work with a partner or group when asked. They sit and do nothing, or they do the task alone. One response might be to give one handout per group or pair. This obliges students to share and work together (and saves paper).

Challenge: Students know that the teacher does not have time to check each group's work, so many of them do not bother to do the task. In this case, make it clear that you will randomly call on several pairs or groups to report their results at the end of an activity. Alternatively, the results of their work must be written in English for collecting and marking.

Challenge: If the task is interesting and students become engaged in it, they forget about speaking English. If students are using too much of their first language during pair or group work, ask them to set a goal for second language use during activities. Later, ask them to evaluate whether they met their goal or ask group members to evaluate each other. Another idea is to assign a second language monitor in each group to keep group members focused on speaking English. In many cases, some use of the first language can be tolerated as long as students are on task and must talk about and produce something in English by the end of the activity.

Students' Attitudes and Expectations

Challenge: Students' main concern is passing the end-of-year exam, which tests grammar and reading comprehension. They, their parents, and the school administration do not see the value of learning to actually communicate in English. Passing end-of-year exams is naturally a very real concern. Show students sample questions from a previous exam which demonstrate that communicative activities will, in the end, increase their command of the language and help them pass the exam. In addition, when introducing new methods, it is best to do so gradually. Moving slowly from known, comfortable methods to new ones gives teachers and students alike more time to adjust (Lewis, 1996).

Challenge: When students are asked to do pair work, they only want to work with their friends. If asked to work with a new partner, they refuse. Encourage students to show their respect for others by listening to what they have to say in group work or other situations. You can encourage cooperation by making it clear that everyone must work with various classmates, which will give them a chance to work with their old friends as well as to make new ones.

Challenge: When students are asked to work in pairs or groups, the stronger students do all the work and the weaker ones do little or nothing. To solve this problem, design activities in which all students must contribute to the final outcome (e.g., jigsaw, information gap). Or turn this problem into an advantage by giving more advanced students responsibility for helping others as group leaders, monitors, or teaching assistants. Make it their responsibility to see that everyone participates. Another idea is to assign roles to group members so that everyone in the group is involved. Roles should be rotated among group members, with different students acting as the facilitator, secretary, recorder, timekeeper, and so on.

Lack of Resources

Challenge: Students have no books, the teacher has limited or no access to resources, or there is no electricity. The only items in the classroom are a blackboard and chalk. Rather than writing notes on the board for students to copy, try more interesting ways of getting necessary information into their notebooks. For example, dictate information using *dictogloss:* Students listen twice to a passage read at normal speed, taking notes during the second reading, and then work with a partner to try to reconstruct the text. When a pair thinks they have it, they write the passage on the board and the class works together to make it as close to the original as possible. You make the final corrections, and the students correct their work (Wajnryb, 1990). Here are a few additional responses to this challenge:

- To save time during class, write texts or questions on large sheets of newsprint before class rather than writing on the board during class.

- Use pictures from magazines or learn to draw simple pictures in order to illustrate vocabulary or generate interest in activities (an excellent resource is Wright, 1994).

- Bring (or ask students to bring) realia—physical objects that language learners can see, hear, and touch—into the classroom. You can generate a great deal of interest when you pull surprising things out of a bag!

- Use students themselves as input—for instance, what they are wearing for names of clothing, how tall or short they are for comparatives and superlatives, or where they are sitting for prepositions of place. What students say can also be used as input. For example, to practice changing direct to indirect speech, a student can be asked a question and another student asked to report what was said.

Motivating Students in Multilevel Classes

Challenge: Students are not really interested in learning English. It is a required subject that is not relevant to their lives. At the beginning of the year, provide students with information about the importance of English as a world language. Encourage them to brainstorm reasons for learning English and the advantages of being able to speak another language. Ask students to think of all the places they hear or read English in their lives.

    Challenge: In a large class, it is easy for students to feel alienated. If they think that the teacher does not know or care whether they learn, they may put little effort into participating actively in the learning process. One response is to create a seating chart to help you learn students' names. When you know and use their names, students feel more like individuals and are more likely to be engaged. Another strategy for learning names is to have students make name cards to display on their desks. Also, as much as possible, be available to students before and after class to provide extra help and establish personal relationships so that they feel they are individuals in the eyes of the teacher, not merely part of the "herd."

Challenge: Different students are at different levels—some are true beginners and others are at an intermediate level or higher. Either the lower level students are lost or the higher level students are bored. To address this issue, plan a variety of activities that appeal to students of different levels who have a variety of learning styles and interests. Variety can often keep the attention of the majority of students. To keep more advanced students challenged, prepare a resource notebook and keep it in the classroom. Students who finish activities quickly can take advantage of enjoyable extras while waiting for the rest of the class to finish. Along the same lines, include "extra challenge" activities such as puzzles or riddles on worksheets or written exercises so that students who finish early can have something to do. One final idea is to develop sequential activities with several steps. Higher level students will be able to complete more steps, lower level students fewer steps—the point is that the sequence allows them to work at their own pace.

CURRICULUM, TASKS, MATERIALS

Taking into consideration our five characteristics for successful speaking activities, along with our list of challenges and possible solutions in teaching speaking in large classes, a creative teacher can implement a variety of successful oral activities. In this section, we give several examples from our own experience. We hope these activities will activate your thinking about other possibilities that encourage active participation by all students in multilevel classes both large and small.

Activity 1: Describing Pictures

Objective: Students will be able to describe a picture and identify a picture from descriptions by other students.

Materials: One picture for each group of four to five students (These could be enlarged photographs, pictures from magazines, or drawings made by the teacher or students. They must be big enough to be seen from across the classroom.)

Level: Beginner

Procedure:

1. Divide students into groups by asking students in one row to turn around to face those in the row behind them. Then each group sends one person to the front of the classroom to choose a picture from the teacher's desk.

2. Give students 5 minutes to look at their picture. Individually, they brainstorm words that name or describe things in the picture. They share their words with the group and together choose five words that best describe what they see. One student writes down the selected words.

3. Collect the pictures, and redistribute them so that each group has a new picture. Give the groups a few minutes to look at and discuss the new pictures.

4. One member of each group reads the words that the group chose to describe their original picture. When a group hears their new picture being described, they hold up the picture and ask, "Is this it?" If a group identifies a picture correctly, they are given one point. If not, the words are read again until a group identifies the correct picture.

Variations: More advanced students can use sentences rather than words to describe the pictures.

Activity 2: Things in Common

Objective: Students will be able to express things they have in common using the expressions *we both have* and *we both are.*

Materials: None

Level: Beginner and above

Procedure:

1. Model the activity with a student by listing things that you like or dislike. The student answers, "So do I" or "I don't."

2. After presenting the term *in common,* make a list on the board of things that you have in common with the student and presents the stem *we both have/are.*

3. Students work in pairs to find out as many things as they can that they have in common. These should be things that are not visible and can only be discovered through asking and answering questions. They write down as many sentences as they can that begin with "We both have/are."

4. Each pair shares their sentences with another pair.

5. Ask several students to say what their classmates said that they had in common.

Variations: For more advanced-level students, pairs can ask each other *wh*-questions to find what they have in common with their partners.

Activity 3: Similes for Learning

Objective: Working in a group, students will be able to brainstorm ideas, choose the best simile, and present it to the class.

Materials: Common objects brought by the teacher or collected from students

Level: Advanced beginner or higher

Procedure:

1. Collect as many items as possible from around the classroom, or bring common items (e.g., rubber band, glue stick, paper clip, marker, piece of chalk, eraser, book, blank paper, battery), and spread them out at the front of the room.

2. Write on the board, "Learning English is like a _____ because _____." Then provide examples such as "Learning English is like a rubber band because there is no beginning or end" or "Learning English is like a rubber band because it can stretch and hold many things together."

3. Each group of three to five students sends one person to the front to choose an item.

4. Groups are given 3–5 minutes to think of as many similes as possible using their item. They discuss their ideas and choose the best simile to present to the rest of the class.

5. Each group presents their simile to the class, and the class votes on the best one. The winning simile can be written on a poster and displayed in the classroom.

Variations: Other topics can be used, for example, "School is like _____" and "Christmas is like _____."

Activity 4: Elicited Dictation (adapted from Hess, 2001)

Objective: Students will be able to express preferences orally and in writing and do peer correction on their written work.

Materials: Paper and pencils

Level: Advanced beginner and above

Procedure:

1. Elicit or give a topic (e.g., fast food, school subjects, clothes, movies).

2. Students divide their paper into three columns with the headings *Agree, Disagree,* and *Not Sure.*

3. Provide a short sentence about the topic (e.g., "Fast food is good for you"). Students write it in one of the columns according to their opinion.

4. Elicit several sentences from students who volunteer their opinions on the topic. Students also write these sentences in the column of their choice.

5. Students compare papers with a partner and discuss their reasons for agreeing or disagreeing with the opinions expressed or with one another.

6. Students look at one another's sentences, comparing spelling, punctuation, and capitalization. They discuss differences and ask you for correction or clarification if necessary.

Activity 5: The Blank Piece of Paper (adapted from Thornbury, 2003)

Objective: Students will be able to reproduce a story they have heard and create their own story.

Materials: Blank piece of paper

Level: All

Procedure:

1. Hold up a blank sheet of paper, and tell the class that you will describe, for example, a recent vacation.

2. Students listen to the descriptive story, for example: "I went to the mountains of Vermont for my vacation. In this picture, you can see my husband, my two children, and me on the top of a mountain. Although it is summer, it is very cold, so we are wearing warm clothes. There are clouds in the sky, and we hope it won't rain. It's so cold that it might even snow. The view is wonderful, and below us we can see a small town with a church, a park, and a river."

3. Working in pairs, students use a blank piece of paper to retell your story.

4. One pair comes to the front and retells the story. Other students collaborate to add missing details.

5. Students tell their own stories with imaginary pictures to a small group, adapting or repeating these steps.

REFLECTIONS

Looking back at the characteristics of a good speaking activity outlined at the beginning of the chapter, it is easy to see that these five activities meet the criteria:

1. The students talk quite a bit. The activities require student engagement and motivate students to speak in the target language.

2. Participation is even. In order to succeed, all members of the group must contribute.

3. Motivation is high because these activities call on students to contribute something of themselves, their interests and their lives, their culture and their society. Like most people, students enjoy talking about themselves and will usually do so quite willingly.

4. These activities are adaptable and can easily be changed to suit the various levels of the students.

5. The activities are goal oriented. They have clear objectives, and there is always some kind of closure that allows students and teacher to judge how successfully the task has been completed.

Each of these activities can be done in large multilevel classes. In our work in Haiti, we have either done these activities or seen them done in crowded classrooms with 50 or more students. Teachers have shown us that by introducing communicative speaking activities gradually into their traditional courses, and by giving students the opportunity to learn behaviors that are suited to their situation, these activities can be used successfully. When given the chance to take responsibility for their learning and to contribute something of themselves to the class, students participate actively and with enthusiasm. Discipline problems are minimized when student motivation is high and when students feel that they are making progress in their learning. Our experience has convinced us that communicative methods can be used successfully in large classes, even where resources are limited.

In conclusion, we offer this story of one of our Haitian teachers. Franz gets on the bus near his home at 5 a.m. every day to get to his class at the government secondary school by 7:30 a.m. This morning, he is carrying three posters that he created last night. Because the school does not have any books or materials for him to use in teaching his Secondary 2 English class of 80 students, he creates his own materials when he has time. He will put up these posters at different places in the classroom so that all the students can see them.

Today his topic is the simple past tense. Students need to know how to form this tense as part of the final exam in order to pass to the next level, and Franz knows that many students have problems with irregular forms of past-tense verbs. He also knows that they have studied the past-tense forms before but have never tried to use these grammatical features to communicate.

When Franz arrives in his classroom, there is quite a bit of noise from his students and from the surrounding classes. Each classroom faces onto a courtyard, and the younger kids are playing there. As students enter Franz's classroom, they take their name cards from a large box and go to their assigned seats. He can tell who is absent based on which name tags are left.

Students follow the instructions that Franz has written on the cracked chalkboard: "Get in your assigned groups. Divide into the following roles: facilitator, English monitor, secretary, timekeeper." He has placed students in their current groups for a period of 2 weeks. They now know each other fairly well and are willing to take turns with roles that have also become familiar. They discussed reasons and rules for working together at the beginning of the semester, and Franz often reminds them of these rules. He gives students 3 minutes to arrange themselves into groups; then he raises his hand and waits for students to also raise their hands, a signal for silence that he has established with the class.

Franz then introduces the task: writing a group story in the past tense. To motivate the more reluctant students, he reminds them that they will need to know the forms of past-tense verbs in order to pass the government exam. He invites them to look at the posters placed around the room. Each poster contains 10 verbs in the present tense. The students are to decide in their groups what the past-tense forms of these verbs are. Several minutes later, Franz does a quick check with the whole class to make sure that most students know the correct forms. He then gives each group's secretary a piece of paper. These students are to write down a story that their group creates in the past tense using their 10 verbs (in any order). The story will feature two characters, Mary and Jacques, a brother and sister who have a 2-day holiday from school and are going to visit a relative in another town. Franz has tried giving students a more open-ended framework, but he finds that more control over the topic helps students focus on the verbs rather than spending too much time trying to figure out a storyline. This topic is one to which most students can relate and for which the verbs make more sense. He tells students to write three paragraphs, an instruction that controls the amount of material and helps students improve the quality of their writing. They have 15 minutes to create the story, after which they pass their story to another group to make corrections.

Franz moves around the room, providing help to students who need it. He has to remind several groups to try to use English and not Creole in their conversations. He also has to remind one group to work together because he sees that each student in the group is busy writing his or her own story. In another group, one student seems to be doing all the work, so Franz reminds this group to work cooperatively as well. After the 15 minutes are up, he redistributes the papers to new groups to read the story and make corrections, but only of the verb forms.

Franz next asks students to say and spell the correct past-tense form of each verb and writes it on the board. He then chooses one of the stories and reads it aloud to the class, asking students to raise their hands when they hear one of the verbs. He does a quick comprehension check by asking questions about the group's story. The next day he will read additional stories, and by the end of the week he will have read aloud every story. He does not have time to make corrections on each story and return it, but by reading the stories aloud he can evaluate where the major problems are and assess whether students have learned the past-tense forms. After all the stories have been read by him and perhaps by advanced-level students, Franz returns the stories and pairs groups to share their stories one more time. When the bell rings, he collects the stories so that they will be ready to use at the beginning of the next class. If he has time tonight, he will read them through quickly to assess the students' work and decide where to begin the next day.

ACKNOWLEDGMENTS

Many of the ideas in this chapter and in a previous article (Renaud, Tannenbaum, & Stantial, 2007) originated from the teachers we worked with in Haiti, to whom we are sincerely grateful.

Susan Donnelly Renaud was a Soros Foundation English teacher trainer in Haiti for 7 years. She has taught English and trained English language teachers in the United States, Africa, Eastern Europe, and Asia. She currently works as a trainer for the SIT Graduate Institute TESOL Certificate Program, in Brattleboro, Vermont, in the United States.

Elizabeth Tannenbaum is an associate professor in the MAT Program at the SIT Graduate Institute, in Brattleboro, Vermont, in the United States. She teaches methodology and applied linguistics courses. She has trained teachers in the United States, Asia, the South Pacific, and Haiti.

Michael Jerald has spent his career as a language teacher and teacher educator. He recently retired after 28 years as a faculty member in the SIT Graduate Institute's MAT Program. He continues to teach courses there and conduct other intensive ESOL teacher training programs.

CHAPTER 5

Every Student Wins: Using "Team English" With Large Multilevel Classes in Thailand

Marguerite G. MacDonald and Ian L. Smith

Multilevel classes can be challenging for any teacher. They are particularly daunt-ing for the English as a foreign language (EFL) or English as an international language (EIL) teacher, who is often responsible for a classroom of 40, 60, 100, or more students (see, e.g., Al-Jarf, 2006; Allwright, 1989; Coleman, 1989; Palmer, 1999; Peng, 2007). Small groups offer a way to personalize multilevel classes by providing opportunities for students to mentor each other and for teachers to individualize instruction (see, e.g., Bell, 1994; Hemingway, 1986; Rinvolucri, 1986; Stein, 1997). Group activities generally allow more interaction than do whole-class activities, with the accompanying advantage of creating a more natural environment for communicative language.

Although the use of small groups can be quite beneficial in large classes, the practice also poses several challenges. Teachers may be awkward with or overwhelmed by unfamiliar methodology, students may lack experience with group work, available materials may not be designed for small groups, and, most challenging, the use of groups can make classroom management quite difficult (LoCastro, 2001). Faced with these challenges, EFL/EIL teachers may be tempted to avoid group work and maintain a traditional classroom organization (Gahin & Myhill, 2003; McKay, 2003).

Because groups in large multilevel classes can be difficult to organize and monitor, they must be designed so that they take minimal time to arrange and provide maximum accountability. In this chapter, we describe Team English, a framework that can assist teachers in managing groups while motivating students to learn and practice. We document a pilot project in which Team English was introduced into the English classrooms of a rural school in southeast Thailand. Using this framework, Thai teachers are beginning to shift from a traditional teacher-fronted classroom to a more student-centered learning environment in which students work together for the success of all.

Team English was created by the first author of this chapter, Marguerite G. MacDonald, to provide a structure that addresses the challenges and promotes the benefits of using small groups in large multilevel classes. It was first piloted at a private school in Thailand (MacDonald, Thiravithul, Butkulwong, & Kednoi, 2002) and later introduced into teacher training by Zena (Thiravithul) Tarasena, who, together with MacDonald, further developed the concept. Ian L. Smith, this chapter's second author and the leader of the pilot project described here, learned of Team English and began using it for teacher training in Thailand, further advancing the concept and its implementation. Under the auspices of the Teacher Plus Foundation, the ongoing Team English pilot project is being conducted at Ban Chamkho School in Thailand. This chapter focuses primarily on the semester from May to September 2007.

Team English is an organizational and motivational framework that incorporates principles of cooperative learning. Teachers adapt their activities for the Team English classroom. By remaining with the same team over a period of several months, student teammates develop loyalty to each other, which motivates every member to succeed and to see that the other members succeed as well.

Team English expands on many of the components that have been recommended for group work in large classes: teams, permanent groups, peer tutoring, color coding, competition, and points. Unique to Team English are the numbered, color-coded uniforms that all students wear. Much as in sports, the colors and numbers allow easy identification of teams and specific team members. They also facilitate organizing and implementing activities. Team English is likewise unique in creating a second layer of organization within the team. Just as universities are divided into colleges and then departments, and countries into states or provinces and then districts or counties, Team English has two layers of organization. Classes are divided into teams, which can then be further divided into subgroups (as in Figure 1). This creates greater structure in the classroom and more student accountability.

Without this secondary layer of organization, large classes employ too many small groups or the groups become unmanageably large. A classroom with too many groups becomes chaotic, with the teacher finding it difficult to supervise all the groups. If each group is given a turn to share with the class, the activity can consume too much time. In large groups, individual students may feel lost or free to "disappear." Team English provides students with the intimacy and commitment of smaller groups yet engages them as part of a larger team. Even when a group is not called on to participate at the class level, if another group from their team is represented, students still have a stake in the outcome. Because the

Figure 1. Blue Team Divided Into Two Smaller Groups

captain and other designated leaders within the team assume a supervisory role, groups are more likely to stay on task.

CONTEXT

The Ministry of Education in Thailand has made English a required part of the curriculum, starting from the first grade. Minimum contact hours are 2 hours per week for Grades 1–3, 3 hours per week for Grades 4–6, and 4 hours per week for Grades 7–9. In practice, many nonspecialist teachers avoid teaching English because they have little confidence in their own language skills. But this situation has improved recently, as newly graduated English language specialists have been assigned to many schools.

As with all subjects in Thailand, English tends to be delivered almost entirely via decontextualized rote learning. For many students, little or no progress in communicative abilities is made during 9 years of formal schooling. This problem is exacerbated by large class sizes. Classes of 45–50 students are not at all uncommon, so efforts by the Ministry of Education to promote "child-centered learning" have met with little success.

Ban Chamkho is a small rural school located in Rayong Province, in southeast Thailand. The school enrolls more than 300 students and is staffed by about 20 teachers, 2 of whom are specialist English teachers. In addition, there is a community-funded foreign teacher (from the United States).

Ban Chamkho is classified as a "school of expanded education opportunities." This indicates that when the government extended mandatory schooling to the ninth grade, this school was one of the rural schools that were upgraded in terms of offering the newly mandatory higher grades. In this way, children whose parents did not have the means or inclination to send them to large high schools in the main towns would still have the opportunity to complete their schooling.

Although prior to the introduction of Team English all students at the school would have been considered beginner-level, significant level differences existed within each class. For example, among ninth-grade students, the lowest-level learners might have had a vocabulary of 10–20 words, a handful of set phrases, and the ability to name some letters of the alphabet, whereas the most advanced-level students would have had a vocabulary of 500–1,000 words and a high-beginner reading fluency. With Team English, the teachers hoped to change these results so that all students would have a strong foundation in English.

Team English was first introduced at Ban Chamkho in November 2006. Initially, a limited form of it was piloted with one class for each teacher who taught English. A fuller version was implemented across all classes in May 2007. One change was that in this version, team members were numbered, which brought immediate benefits to the organization of activities and classes in general. Because of a lack of valid assessment data, however, it was not possible to list students from highest to lowest ability levels in order to assign them to teams—the preferred approach, which was implemented later.

CURRICULUM, TASKS, MATERIALS

The project leader and teachers at Ban Chamkho have applied Team English to address the school's needs. In this section we describe the components of Team English and how they are used in the Ban Chamkho classroom. We also document the different ways points are awarded. Finally, we present some of the activities that are used within the framework.

Team Structure

Team English teams are larger than the usual groups of 3–6 students, typically ranging from 9 to 15 members and often encompassing smaller subgroups. A variety of groups can be formed within one team. For example, teams of 9 students allow 28 different combinations of three triads within the team. Each team has a more proficient student serving as captain and a range of ability levels represented among the other students. Because of this balance, every team is multilevel, creating the potential for peer mentoring for lower proficiency students. The team structure also permits homogeneous groupings, with appropriate tasks assigned to each ability group. The teacher can then devote special attention to groups that need the most assistance. We recommend creating new teams at midyear to adjust for different rates of progress during the first semester.

Team Identification and Formations

One distinctive feature of Team English is that it provides a visual identification for all students. Using a sports motif, the framework uses color-themed teams. The name of a team can be the color itself or a more creative name based on the color. Ban Chamkho always uses red, blue, green, and yellow, so four sets of color-coded materials can be reused consistently.

Team uniforms are both colored and numbered; colors and numbers are visible from anywhere in the classroom. The uniforms might be sashes, headbands, reinforced plastic cloth cut to slip over the head like an open-sided tank top, or placards of corrugated plastic covered with clear plastic contact paper. The Ban Chamkho project used placards, as seen in Figures 1 and 2.

Each student receives a number corresponding to a proficiency level. This number matches similar levels across all teams. For example, across all teams the captain, team member #1, may be a higher level student, team member #6

Figure 2. Green Team Captain and Vice Captain Distribute Uniforms

a lower level student, and team member #9 a middle-level student. In this way, heterogeneous and homogeneous groupings can be done quickly and efficiently, with the same group formations applying to every team.

Numbering not only allows the teacher to organize students quickly, it also provides for quick identification of any student who is not on task, making both that student and the team accountable. Teams are penalized if a member goes off task. Numbering also allows for several strategies to maximize student participation while ensuring fairness among the teams.

Although Team English usually randomizes the numbers assigned to different ability levels, in some situations sequencing the numbers according to ability may be more practical. For some cultures, a more transparent hierarchy does not necessarily stigmatize the lower level students. This is the case for Ban Chamkho, which sequences the numbers according to the level of ability, from higher to lower. Teachers easily remember that the higher the number, the more mentoring or assistance the student will probably need.

Another pedagogical advantage is that team formations and other multilevel strategies can be made more transparent to the students. In an introductory class, as the teacher assigns numbers to team members, he or she presents an overview of Team English, describing its benefits for higher, middle, and lower level students as well as students' roles and responsibilities within the team. As team formations are introduced, the teacher also explains their purpose, with a particular focus on how a specific configuration formation is designed to encourage participation by all team members. The teacher constantly reminds team leaders of their responsibility to ensure participation as well as mentor and assist lower level teammates.

Classroom Organization

Team English requires that teams work together in an identified space. In crowded classrooms, the teacher creates a map so that each team has its own section. Even if desks are bolted to the floor, students can form different groups in their designated area. The captain should be centrally located as much as possible so that he or she can supervise the team members. Figure 3 shows how to accomplish this in a classroom with fixed seating. Within this seating arrangement, teams are broken into groups of three. By turning to the desk behind them, group members in front can easily work with those in the row behind. Teams can then reconfigure within their designated space to form different group combinations. Periodically, teams can shift to another part of the classroom so that no one team will always be at the front or back of the room.

When the classroom is more spacious, as at Ban Chamkho, many different configurations are possible. Students can gather in lines, circles, double circles, and other formations to participate in activities. Before implementing Team English, the Ban Chamkho project leader noticed that in an unstructured, teacher-fronted classroom, lower level students invariably sat in the back, paying attention

4	5	6
7	8	9
4	5	6
3	1	2
7	8	9

1	2	3	4	5
4	5	6	7	6
3	2	1	8	9
9	3	1	2	4
7	8	Empty Desk	5	6

1	2	3
7	8	9
4	5	6
3	1	2
7	8	9

Figure 3. Team Organization for a Class of 54 Students

only when directly called on. Initial trials of group work alleviated this situation to some extent, but these students often still remained uninvolved and disinterested as their more proficient teammates bunched together, working so quickly that the lower level students could not follow, let alone contribute. To address this situation, the project leader developed several set team formations to encourage more involvement by all students—students were seated in configurations that promoted cooperative learning and peer assistance across proficiency levels. Figure 4 illustrates one of these formations.

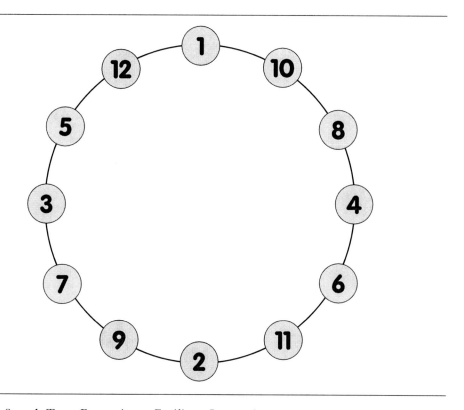

Figure 4. Sample Team Formation to Facilitate Interaction

Another frequently used formation is team coaching, shown in Figures 5 and 6. In this formation, teachers subdivide teams into two groups. For a team of 12, for instance, the team captain (#1) and vice captain (#2) are designated as coaches and sit in front of their respective groups. The least advanced students in each group (#11–12) sit directly in front of the coaches, surrounded by other lower level students (#7–10). Middle level students (#3–6) sit behind the lower level students and are assigned to help and monitor those in front of them and make sure they pay attention.

Team Cohesion

Each team is essentially a small class. For the most part, students operate within their own teams, competing with other teams. Occasionally, however, team members form groups with members of other teams to discover information that they then share with their own team. Individual team members can also compete against individuals from other teams. By remaining a member of the same team for an extended period of time, students experience many of the benefits of a small class. They become comfortable, trusting, and willing to take risks. They

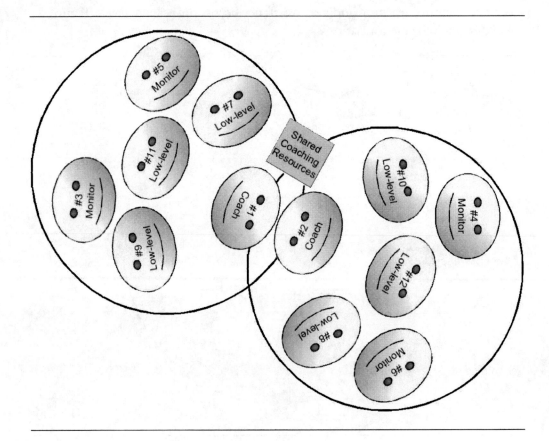

Figure 5. Team Coaching Formation

have a clearer sense of identity and are not lost in a sea of students. They develop team loyalty, as in sports. They understand that success depends not only on their individual efforts but also on the success of all team members. To achieve this, they must help one another.

In terms of achieving success for all team members, team coaching is perhaps the most direct and powerful Team English strategy. Sitting back to back, the coaches share materials, and the teacher walks around the classroom coaching the coaches rather than individual students directly. For example, if team leaders are coaching their teammates in how to tell time, the teacher gives teams clock faces and shows the coaches how to break the task down into manageable parts, practicing hours first, then minutes, then putting the two together.

Team coaching sessions are followed immediately by activities in which teams score points based on the individual performance of team members, thus providing coaches with feedback on the efficacy of their coaching techniques. One example of an activity for this purpose would be a whole-class listening task in which the scores of all team members are averaged to calculate a score for the team. Another example is the Matching Relay activity (described in detail later in the chapter). If time permits, such an activity may be run twice, with a team coaching session between the two rounds. In this case, teams may be awarded bonus points for improving performance the second time around.

Figure 6. Team Coaching in Action

One well-documented problem that team coaching addresses is the relationship between the teacher and lower level students or students with behavior problems. Research shows that teachers who do not feel confident in their teaching have particular difficulties with students who struggle academically or pose disciplinary challenges (see Tournaki & Podell, 2005). The teacher–student relationship can be particularly strained in a language classroom, where anxiety is already high. Teachers can easily become frustrated with students' poor performance and behavior. But in the Team English structure, the teacher and students receive support. The teacher becomes more a referee than a disciplinarian. The captain and other team members assume part of the responsibility for keeping all members on task and promoting student learning. Lower level students are mentored by higher level teammates. Getting help from peers is much less confrontational, and seemingly miraculous changes in student performance and behavior have been observed as a result.

The benefits of such peer support in learning English have been documented for a variety of ages, from kindergarten (Fassler, 1998) to college (Kobayashi, 2003). And team coaching is also beneficial for the coaches. Just as teachers learn more about a subject when they teach it, so too do coaches improve their language skills and gain confidence by mentoring their teammates.

Team Points

Teams compete for points in Team English but with the opportunity for all teams to win various benchmarked rewards as they accumulate points during the course of the term. The teacher awards points for getting materials together for an activity, producing correct answers, quickly completing tasks, following directions, becoming quiet on time, putting materials away, and so forth. The teacher withholds points or penalizes teams for going off task, not becoming quiet on time, making incorrect challenges, and the like. Because points are awarded to or taken away from the entire team, teammates have a strong motivation to keep everyone on task. Teams are intensely competitive in moving from one formation to another, with points awarded to the teams that do so most quickly.

Encouragement Points

For certain activities, the teacher announces that encouragement points apply. This provides even more incentive for higher level students to mentor their lower level teammates because more points are given to lower level students who can do assigned tasks. For example, when teams have 12 members, students #3–6 are awarded one bonus point, students #7–9 two bonus points, and students #10–12 three bonus points. Encouragement points work well in conjunction with team coaching and help the team bonding process.

Graded Task Points

The graded task strategy mirrors encouragement points. It provides an opportunity for more advanced students to challenge themselves and be rewarded appropriately. In certain activities, students are given a choice of level for the task that they wish to attempt. For example, in the Lucky Dip activity (described in detail in the next section), students can draw a card from an "Easy" (1 point), "Medium" (2 points), or "Difficult" (3 points) container. Team members choose their own level and earn more points for more difficult assignments.

"I Don't Know . . . Help Me, Please" Points

This strategy encourages even the lowest level students to make some attempt at English communication rather than remaining quiet or resorting to their native language. If an activity employs this approach, points are raised by one from their normal levels. For example, scoring for the "Easy," "Medium," and "Difficult" cards from the graded tasks strategy would be raised to 2, 3, and 4 points, respectively. This leaves room to award a single point if a student informs the class that he or she cannot recall the answer and then asks for help from a more proficient teammate in order to be able to answer correctly.

Important to this strategy is that the more advanced teammates cannot answer on behalf of the lower level ones, but must whisper the answer. To earn the point, lower level students must give the answer themselves. Also important is that 1 point is the maximum awarded for this exchange; otherwise, students might deliberately select tasks above their level, acting as a proxy for better teammates. In addition to encouraging communication, the 1-point contribution to the team's score builds the confidence and self-esteem of lower level students, often resulting in their performance improving well beyond expectations, surprising teachers, classmates, and themselves in the process.

Teamwork Points

The teacher conducts a 5-minute feedback session at the end of each class, during which each team is awarded points for teamwork during the lesson. All students are reminded of their responsibilities to their teams. If students have been noticed as going off task, fewer points are awarded and the whole team, rather than individual students, must take responsibility for the lower score. Conversely, the team is rewarded with more points if students have managed to keep all members on task during a lesson.

Because students in Ban Chamkho have been so motivated by winning points, tangible rewards have not been developed beyond simple classroom privileges. It is planned, though, that a coupon system will be implemented later, enabling students to cash in accumulated coupons for actual rewards.

Team Activities

Team English is used to implement a variety of activities. The following two popular activities illustrate how Team English facilitates inclusive turn-taking in a multilevel class.

Matching Relay

This activity can be used to practice vocabulary recognition in reading, writing, listening, and speaking. Two tables for each team are set up at opposite ends of the classroom. A set of written vocabulary cards is placed face down on one table; matching picture cards are arranged face up on the opposite table. Teams are stationed around the tables. One student from each team must run to the opposite table, pick up a vocabulary card, read it, and call out the word to his or her teammates. The rest of the team must locate the corresponding picture card. Then one team member runs with that card and hands it to the teammate at the opposite table. That student clips the two cards together and returns to the main group while the student who brought the picture card picks up a new vocabulary card, and the process repeats.

For this activity to involve all students, it is important to control turn-taking. More advanced students will want to take turn after turn in an effort to win more points, and because this game is so vigorous, under normal circumstances it would be almost impossible to keep track of turn-taking. However, with numbered uniforms it becomes easy. Teams are told that turn-taking must follow the numbers. If team members are observed failing to go in order, they are penalized or disqualified.

Lucky Dip

This activity can be used to address many areas such as phonics improvement, vocabulary building, and grammatical development, including singular/plural, demonstratives (*this/these/that/those*), tenses, and so forth. The activity is conducted much like a game show, with the teacher performing the role of host (see Figure 7). As with Matching Relay, this activity uses two sets of corresponding cards. Depending on students' ability level, and which skills the teacher wishes to practice, both sets of cards may contain pictures, both sets text, or one set each of pictures and text. One student picks a random card from one set, identifies the word or phrase that the card represents, and calls it out. The teams must listen for the item, collaboratively choose the corresponding card from the other set, and send it to the teacher.

Turn-taking in the Lucky Dip activity works on two levels: one for listening and one for speaking. For listening, a number is selected for the corresponding student on each team to take responsibility for identifying the answer for that round. The number may be chosen deliberately by the teacher, drawn by raffle, or left to the team captain to decide. Although all team members cooperate to

Figure 7. Red Team Celebrating a Lucky Dip Win

choose or formulate an answer, it is the selected team member's responsibility to make the final decision and bring the answer card to the teacher. If the teacher notices that the better students are dominating the process and simply handing the card to the designated student to take to the teacher, they are reminded of the teamwork points that will be awarded (or not) at the end of the lesson. Turn-taking for the students designated to call out the word or phrase works on a longer cycle. For example, if #11 is selected for a round, then a complete round consists of the #11 member from each team coming up to take a turn. This is important to ensure fairness across the teams.

REFLECTIONS

The Ban Chamkho pilot project represented the first cycle of fully implementing Team English, and two major problems were encountered. The first was the composition of one team. Due to incomplete testing data, the team captain was inappropriately selected. The teachers and project leader realized that this situation should have been addressed early on rather than allowed to continue through the cycle. The teams were reorganized for the second cycle, as valid assessment data was then available, which also reflected the different degrees of progress among the students during the first cycle. The second problem involved lower level students. Teachers felt that these students were still not receiving the full benefits of Team English, so new activities were introduced, with more individual responsibility, and greater emphasis was placed on team coaching to address the needs of these students.

Overall, though, the first cycle was quite successful, engaging all students and providing opportunities for peer mentoring. This success has led to the expansion of Team English to other schools. Following the first cycle, teachers from the region were brought to Ban Chamkho for training in implementing Team English. As a result, small-scale Team English projects were implemented in three other schools in the Rayong area. More schools were invited to join the network in early 2008. Additionally, the Teacher Plus Foundation appointed a project leader to head a similar effort in Ubon Province, in northeast Thailand.

One reason that Team English has been more effective than other attempts at group work in Ban Chamkho is that unlike many types of group work, including those used in more traditional forms of cooperative learning, Team English uses a built-in sports hierarchy, a structure that exists nearly worldwide. Participation in group work then becomes more acceptable for students and teachers alike, providing an easier transition from traditional teacher-fronted classrooms to learner-centered groups. Being a member of a team reinforces students' responsibility to do their part and not tune out, as often happens in teacher-fronted classrooms. Therefore, the advantages of groups are combined with a familiar hierarchy. Team English is especially helpful for lower level classes, in which traditional group approaches are often difficult to implement.

As the Ban Chamkho project illustrates, Team English provides large multi-level classrooms with a structure that shifts the focus to students. It is particularly effective for EFL/EIL classrooms, where such a shift has sometimes been difficult for teachers as well as students. Team English facilitates organization of the classroom for peer mentoring and promotes maximum participation by all students while maintaining order. The pilot project at Ban Chamkho illustrates how, even with very limited English skills, students can fully participate in classroom activities, gaining language skills, confidence, and enthusiasm to develop their English proficiency further. When students become more advanced in English, groups can become more autonomous and communicative, further developing the linguistic and social skills necessary for effective communication. Although competition drives the Team English classroom, in the end every student wins.

Marguerite G. MacDonald is the Frederick A. White Distinguished Professor of Professional Service and director of TESOL Programs at Wright State University, in Dayton, Ohio, in the United States, where she teaches linguistics and TESOL pedagogy. She created Team English to address the difficulty of working with groups in large classes and first introduced it in Thailand in 2000–2001.

Ian L. Smith is a teacher trainer and project leader in Rayong, Thailand, for the Teacher Plus Foundation. Having worked in Thailand since 1992, he currently focuses on developing communicative, learner-centered language teaching practices in rural Thai schools.

Spurring Creativity and Imagination

CHAPTER 6

Go to Commercial: Using Television Commercials in Multilevel EFL Classrooms

Frank Tuzi, Ann Junko Young, and Keiko Mori

Television commercials are fun, persuasive, and memorable acts of communication that not only can capture the attention of language learners but also can be used to stimulate them to think critically about deeper linguistic and cultural meanings. The literature on TV commercials describes how to use them in language classrooms, the advantages of doing so, and how to find and select them. But until recently, using television commercials was an arduous task because of the difficulty of acquiring them. Before the Internet and TiVo, finding and preparing commercials for classroom use required a great deal of time; today, they are easily obtained in digital format, making their preparation and use easier. With the difficulties of acquiring commercials eliminated, teachers can begin incorporating them into their multilevel or mixed-ability curricula.

As teachers, we know that no matter how carefully a school tries to divide students into different levels of language ability, discrepancies in language learning goals, learning styles, educational backgrounds, and levels of motivation are always present in every classroom. These variations are further aggravated when students of different language proficiency levels coexist in one class. Besides struggling to organize a syllabus so as to achieve a shared set of goals, teachers also have the difficult task of selecting materials that can be used by all students at the same time. TV commercials can aid in satisfying the needs of multilevel or mixed-ability classes because their visual qualities greatly increase students' comprehension.

This chapter explains how to make use of this treasure trove of resources in order to take advantage of these authentic materials in a multilevel or mixed-ability second language (L2) classroom. First we summarize research and benefits, and then we share how TV commercials provide rich opportunities to teach language, culture, values, and critical thinking in ways that encourage interaction and increase motivation. We also describe how to incorporate commercials into an L2 curriculum, including specific tasks or activities for use in multilevel classrooms.

CONTEXT

What the Researchers Say

A small group of TV commercial researchers and users have been recommending commercials as language learning tools for years; however, this resource never really took root in the L2 classroom (Davis, 1997; Erkaya, 2005; Smith & Rawley, 1997). A major reason for the lack of enthusiasm, as previously mentioned, was the difficulty of acquiring the commercials in forms that could be easily used in the classroom. Thanks to technological advances, however, their usefulness and accessibility today make them a valuable tool in the L2 teacher's toolbox.

The majority of existing studies on the impact and effectiveness of TV commercials in English as a foreign language consists of classroom research and educators' personal experiences (Davis, 1997; Goldthorpe, 1993; Katchen, 1993; F. Lee, 1994). One positive finding is that students exposed to these commercials in the classroom improve their listening skills or that their motivation to listen increases at a faster rate than that of students who only experience listening to audio (Davis, 1997; F. Lee, 1994). Lee's students of Chinese as a second language, for example, improved their listening skills through video. After 60 hours of listening materials, the control group (audio only) understood less because fewer cues were available to them. Poon (1992) conducted similar research, however, and did not see a significant improvement, though students who watched TV news clips did claim that they were more motivated than students who only listened to the news. These few studies give positive indications but do not provide a significant basis for large claims or generalizations about the benefits of TV commercials. More research is needed. Davis rightly states that commercials were an untapped resource; they remain a largely untapped resource today.

In addition to providing rich content, TV commercials can aid in teaching critical analysis skills. McGee and Fujita (2000) focused on the ability of commercials to enhance critical thinking skills. They provided students with modeling and critical analysis training, and using commercials, students reviewed the models and practiced analyzing the culture and intentions of the commercials. Students also viewed and wrote about commercials on their own. McGee and Fujita's findings seem to indicate that commercials are a useful tool for developing awareness and analysis of cultural differences as well as building critical thinking skills in response to advertising.

Reasons for Using Television Commercials

Despite the limited research, there are a number of reasons for using TV commercials. Both Davis (1997) and Erkaya (2005) recommend using them as short, authentic texts that encourage cultural understanding and critical thinking. Unlike TV shows or movies, commercials do not inundate students with information. Their visual clues provide scaffolding to help students understand linguistic meanings. Additionally, their brevity makes them easier for teachers to select, manipulate, and prepare for classroom use.

The authenticity and depth of TV commercials are also advantages in the classroom. By using commercials from a variety of locations, language teachers can introduce different accents, dialects, cultures, and values. The variety of voices that commercials can provide is far greater than listening materials that accompany typical textbooks. The cultural and values elements can be used as a springboard to language practice and critical analysis.

It is also important to remember that TV commercials are designed to be attractive and fun, and to motivate viewers to purchase goods or services. L2 students will enjoy these 15- to 60-second bits of culture because most of them were designed to be enjoyed. How many times have you found yourself repeating a song or phrase from a commercial? This entertainment value is another benefit and a reason to recommend their use in L2 classrooms. Finally, commercials are especially beneficial to students in situations where access to native speakers and authentic language is limited. Because this kind of context makes it unlikely that students will be able to use English outside the classroom in natural ways, authentic materials such as commercials can make even deeper impacts on students.

Using Television Commercials in Japanese University English Classrooms

Our students were mostly freshmen and sophomores at three universities in the Tokyo area. Class size varied from 10 to 40. Though the students were homogeneous in terms of cultural background, their proficiency and motivational levels varied. Because we were not assigned specific textbooks, we could easily integrate lessons using TV commercials into the course schedule.

Because using TV commercials in the classroom was a new idea to our students, we provided an overview in one of the first lessons. We presented a series of commercials and asked students to take notes about the products, slogans, and other aspects that caught their attention. Many were watching commercials in English for the first time, and they seemed curious to see the images, products, and services being advertised. Because they had Internet access, students were also assigned to browse relevant Web sites where they could choose television commercials for listening and discussing with their classmates (see Appendix A).

As the semester continued, students participated in additional lessons using TV commercials. Each lesson included vocabulary, grammar, pronunciation, listening, and culture and values discussion activities as well as reading and writing activities—a sequence that normally occupied two 90-minute class sessions. (Details of this process are provided later in the chapter.)

CURRICULUM, TASKS, MATERIALS

The curriculum that teachers use should be based on clear and specific goals so that they can find appropriate materials, methods, and forms of assessment (J. C. Richards, 2001). When dealing with mixed-ability students, it is also important that the curriculum meet different students' needs and interests. In a multilevel classroom, a functional or process type of syllabus is generally more effective. A theme-based approach allows a broad range of activities to be included (Bell, 1991).

After a needs analysis is done and the main course goals have been established, teachers can address the challenges of dealing with multilevel classes. We believe that TV commercials can assist language teachers in meeting their curricular goals and objectives, and addressing these challenges. For example, teachers can use different commercials for different levels of groups in the same class, or they can use the same commercial but then focus on different linguistic or cultural elements for the different levels. Teachers can also encourage students to help each other, which would equip lower level students with additional scaffolding, modeling, and needed assistance. For students of all levels, commercials, as short and authentic texts, can stimulate high levels of motivation for learning.

Teaching Pronunciation, Forms, and Lexicon

One of the foundational uses of TV commercials in language classes is to allow teachers to focus on linguistic components in the commercials, such as vocabulary, pronunciation, and structure. Commercials are compressed texts that contain deliberate or scripted vocabulary paired with visual and other audio elements. These carefully chosen words are often repeated to encourage viewers to remember the main points. Thus, commercials are a good way to introduce vocabulary in context along with different connotations. Teachers can also use them as an entry to related content (e.g., a laundry detergent commercial can begin a lesson on clothing or housework).

TV commercials introduce specific grammar structures in their scripts. They typically repeat words and phrases, which encourage meaningful memorization. The key for educators is to find commercials that present the linguistic elements that they wish to focus on in particular courses or lessons.

Beyond these elements of syntax and lexicon, TV commercials provide excellent opportunities to teach listening and speaking. They present countless situations that teachers can use, mimic, or modify to teach speaking patterns, give examples of functions, or create contextualized practice opportunities. Commercials also offer opportunities to study suprasegmentals such as tone, intonation, and accent. Because of their flexibility, commercials are ideal for mixed-ability classes; simpler tasks can be assigned to lower level students and more complex tasks to higher level students. For example, one group of students might work on writing an original script for a commercial while another rehearses or role-plays a scripted commercial's dialogue.

Using the Campbell's Soup commercial script in Figure 1, teachers might focus on commands for lower level students and reported speech for upper level students. This commercial has commands in several forms that lower level students can learn, identify, and model. Teachers can help such learners identify different forms (e.g., "You have to make dinner," "Make something good," "You're doing the dishes") and then build on these examples by providing opportunities to use the structures in class. Similarly, higher level students can study reported speech found in the commercial (e.g., "I thought you were going to be late") and use the samples to identify the structure of reported speech as well as practice using it.

It would be a relatively easy task to create listening and speaking activities using the same commercial. Lower level students might complete a cloze activity while higher level students take dictation. Similarly, lower level students can

Description	Script
Dad arrives home first and listens to the messages on the answering machine. The first message is from his daughter:	Mom, Kate's coming over to dinner. Make something good.
The next message is from his wife:	Bill, I'm stuck at work. You have to make dinner. Good luck!
Dad looks for dinner ideas in his suburban kitchen and grabs a can of mushroom soup. As he prepares dinner, the narrator speaks:	You always knew Campbell's was good. This makes it better: two-step dishes. Just brown chicken, add Campbell's Cream of Mushroom soup, and simmer. So you are only two steps away from a home-cooked meal.
The husband, daughter, and a friend are eating at the dinner table. The wife enters. The husband smiles:	I thought you were going to be late.
The wife, embarrassed, answers:	Did I say that?
The narrator speaks: *Everyone enjoys the dinner and the company.* *The husband speaks:* *The wife makes a face.*	Campbell's two-step dishes. You're doing the dishes.

Figure 1. Sample Commercial: Campbell's Cream of Mushroom Soup

practice performing the commercial, paying close attention to pronunciation and intonation, while higher level students write and perform their own commercial.

The Campbell's Soup commercial contains several functions, including making requests, lying, and giving instructions. The making-requests function would be easier for lower level students to understand and practice, whereas lying and arguing are more complex functions that are more suitable for higher level students.

Teaching Culture

Represented or embedded in all commercials are the originating cultures that developed the ideas to create the commercials. In other words, TV commercials enable instructors to focus on a critical area in teaching language—culture. Commercials are created and constructed within a particular culture and include intended or unintended cultural ideas and values, which can become additional components or springboards in language lessons. We recommend an approach to these issues in line with Seelye's (1993, p. 31) six instructional goals:

1. *Interest:* Students show curiosity about another culture (or another segment or subculture of one's own culture) and empathy toward its members.

2. *Who:* Students recognize that role expectations and other social variables such as age, sex, social class, religion, ethnicity, and place of residence affect the way people speak and behave.

3. *What:* Students realize that effective communication requires discovering the culturally conditioned images that are evoked in the minds of people when they think, act, and react to the world around them.

4. *When-where:* Students recognize that situational variables and convention shape behavior in important ways.

5. *Why:* Students understand that people generally act the way they do because they are using options their society allows for satisfying basic physical and psychological needs and that cultural patterns are interrelated and tend mutually to support need satisfaction.

6. *Exploration:* Students can evaluate a generalization about the target culture in terms of the amount of evidence substantiating it, and they can locate and organize information about the target culture from the library, the mass media, people, and personal observation.

Guided by these goals, teachers can develop activities for different levels of students. These goals can be reached via cultural comparisons, either between the home and target cultures or among target language and regional L2 cultures. Lower level students would typically require more scaffolding and more checking of comprehension, whereas more advanced students could discuss open-ended questions regarding culture, the differences among cultures, and the underlying values of the commercial.

With the Campbell's Soup commercial, for instance, teachers can pique students' curiosity by asking leading questions or facilitating brainstorming about food, cooking, and family roles (Goal 1). They might also investigate gender roles in the family and how these differ between cultures (Goal 3). Students can fill out a worksheet identifying the social variables of the characters (Goal 2; see Appendix B for an example). They might also explore the reasons for the actions in the commercial, such as why the husband cooks the meal or why the friend comes over for a meal (Goal 5). These actions and the reasons for them are not cultural universals.

In addition, teachers can use TV commercials to explore cultural taboos (Goal 5). Certain commercials contain subject matter that may not be acceptable in another culture. Identifying, understanding, and discussing these taboo images, ideas, and values can be an opportunity for meaningful language learning. Teachers and students can explore them and discover the rationales behind them. For instance, it appears that the mother in the commercial may have lied. But lying is a cultural as well as moral concept—what determines a lie and how lying is conducted are culturally distinct elements that students and teachers can investigate via comparative analysis.

Finally, students can attempt to establish generalizations about culture based on information gleaned during their investigations. However, teachers must explain that not all that is seen in commercials represents cultural realities and that students need to find evidence for any generalizations by consulting other sources of information, including people from the target culture, books, articles, and Web sites.

Teaching Critical Thinking

Culture, values, and advertising provide excellent opportunities to focus on critical thinking skills. Despite concerns raised by Atkinson (1997) regarding the teaching of critical thinking in L2, we believe the benefits outweigh any drawbacks. One reason is that it is difficult to separate critical thinking from any form of language use. Additionally, some kind of critical thinking is a universal activity regardless of culture; however, the presentation and content of critical thinking can be different in every culture. To employ TV commercials without thinking critically about their content and values would be a disservice to students.

In this context, teaching critical thinking begins with looking at the TV commercial itself. Commercials have elements that students can evaluate immediately, such as intended audience and main objectives, and teachers can further guide students toward analyzing additional elements such as indirect purposes, nonverbal messages, and lifestyle assumptions. Teachers can also remind students that those who produce commercials are trying to convince or manipulate the audience to buy the product. Their bottom-line goal is to sell a service or product, and students can use this narrow purpose to interpret and analyze the commercial. In this sense, commercials are an excellent resource for multilevel classes. Higher level students can engage in more in-depth reading, research, discussion, and writing while lower level students focus more on simpler questions or issues.

If time, facilities, or equipment make in class use of TV commercials challenging, they can be assigned as homework or for independent study. As with an extensive reading program, students choose what they want to watch from a library of commercials, complete relevant worksheets, and collect them in a portfolio. Teachers evaluate them and give feedback at regular intervals. Another option is to use Internet-based libraries of commercials or have students find and collect commercials to create their own library. (For a list of Web sites, see Appendix A.)

Developing TV Commercial–Based Materials

There are a number of ways that materials developers can proceed when creating materials based on TV commercials. Materials writers normally proceed from a needs analysis and develop materials to meet linguistic, communicative, and cultural needs. However, it can be difficult to find one commercial that meets all of the perceived needs, so Katchen (1993) suggests turning the tables—selecting a good clip first, then building appropriate activities around it. Whichever starting point materials writers choose, they need to understand the needs and interests of students, have an idea of students' access to TV commercials, and use their full creativity to integrate the commercial with linguistically productive tasks and activities.

For mixed-ability classes, we recommend using TV commercials that contain simple linguistic structures and complex sociocultural issues. The antidrug commercial showing a searing hot frying pan in which an egg is cooking is a good example. The script is simple: "This is drugs. This is your brain on drugs. Any questions?" The sociocultural issue, on the other hand, is complex and makes a great discussion topic for higher level learners.

Another element used to select effective commercials is the amount and type of cultural information. Teachers looking to teach cultural elements or contrast them among cultures should search for culturally distinctive or engaging materials and find multiple commercials showing the same cultural elements from different perspectives. The selection process can become quite complex because there is such an array of elements and issues to consider. This is another reason why some teachers choose to mold their objectives around a good commercial instead of the other way around.

REFLECTIONS

Delving into the world of TV commercials and trolling for possible materials for our classes has been an interesting and eye-opening experience. In attempting to incorporate commercials, we have learned much about the process and its potential pitfalls, and we would be remiss if we did not share here our reflections on lessons learned.

The most daunting task for us initially was discovering resources. It took some time to find the best Web sites, not to mention selecting appropriate commercials, downloading them, and developing activities and materials to go along with them. As is often the case with technology, we also found it wise to have a backup plan ready, in case Web sites were temporarily shut down, files were corrupted, or similar problems occurred.

We surveyed our students about the TV commercials in order to improve on their effectiveness. Students commented that they enjoyed the commercial-based lessons and activities, which is an important step for increasing motivation to learn. They also reported acquiring language learning strategies through the use of commercials, such as how to learn language by noticing language being used, how to perceive cultural and value differences, and how to develop critical analysis skills.

One obstacle was the challenge facing those of us who are nonnative-English-speaking teachers. It was a bit challenging for us to work with these authentic materials, but TV commercials became a tool through which we as well as our learners increased our cultural understanding. So the multilevel benefits of commercials extended to the teachers as well.

TV commercials can provide a treasure trove of language learning opportunities. They are easily accessible and often free. They provide not only jumping-off points for learning discrete linguistic and lexical items, but also an avenue for exploring culture and values. Though research studies on the impact and effectiveness of commercials in foreign language education are limited, we believe our classroom experiences justify further research on their use and impact on language learning, cultural awareness, and critical thinking.

Frank Tuzi is associate professor and director of e-learning at Tokyo Christian Institute, in Japan, where he teaches ESL, English composition, and computers. His research interests include second language acquisition, e-learning, and program development.

Ann Junko Young teaches at Bunkyo University and Rikkyo University, in Japan. Her research interests include intercultural education, second language reading and writing, and materials development.

Keiko Mori teaches at Tokyo Christian Institute, in Japan. Her research interests include learner motivation, autonomy in language learning, and English for specific purposes for Christian ESL programs.

APPENDIX A: ANNOTATED LIST OF WEB SITES FOR TELEVISION COMMERCIALS

http://www.veryfunnyads.com

    This site includes commercials from around the globe, many in English.

http://www.apple.com/trailers

    This site has dozens of movie trailers for recent releases.

http://www.esm.psu.edu/faculty/gray/movies.html

    This page includes dozens of Apple commercials.

http://www.movieflix.com/genre_list.php?genre=Commercials

    Movieflix houses a database of video clips that contains a small repository of TV commercials.

http://www.teacheroz.com/retro.htm

    Classic TV commercials from the 1950s and 1960s are included in this online collection of materials.

http://www.stupidvideos.com

    Although no actual commercials are typically housed here, there are a number of excellent commercial parodies and educational clips.

http://www.youtube.com

    This is the mother lode of Web-based video clips. In addition to countless commercials, there are clips for almost any occasion.

http://x-entertainment.com/downloads

    This site includes dozens of commercials from the 1980s. They are not at a high resolution, but they are all free to download.

APPENDIX B: TV COMMERCIAL WORKSHEET

Brand or company name: _____

Product or service: _____

Year: _____

Setting: _____

People who appear in the commercial

Age: _____

Sex: _____

Social class (if applicable): _____

Religion (if applicable): _____

Ethnicity (if applicable): _____

Context in which the people appear

When: _____

Where: _____

How: _____

Target audience

Age: _____ children ____ teenagers _____ adults _____ elderly _____ any age

Gender: _____ male _____female _____ both

Marital status: _____ single _____ married _____ both

_____ Large, general audience _____ Small, regional audience

_____ Business (industrial, trade, professional)

_____ Noncommercial (government, civic groups, religious groups)

Check the items below that apply:

_____ Humorous _____ Serious _____ Exciting _____ Sad

_____ Monologue _____ Dialogue

First impressions

What is the first thing that caught your attention? Why?

Vocabulary

Positive words:
Negative words:
Verbs:
Idioms or set phrases:

Values

What does the commercial suggest that the product provides? Select the three most important items, and explain why.

___ Satisfaction of a physical need	___ Health	___ Sensuality
___ Faster/more efficient service	___ Romance	___ Social authority
___ Better self-image/life	___ Friendship	___ Better price
___ Safety	___ Power	___ Easy use
___ Status	___ Glamour	___ Better quality
___ Enjoyment/happiness	___ Time	___ New identity
___ Comfort	___ Money	___ Idea

Pros and cons for buying the product

According to this commercial, what will happen in the following situations?

If I buy this product or use this service, I _____

If I don't buy this product or use this service, I _____

Critical analysis

Do you think this commercial would be successful in your country? Why or why not?

If not, how might you change it?

CHAPTER 7

Photography as a Cultural Text for Language Learning

Walter Gene Pleisch and Joel See

The proverb "A picture is worth a thousand words" holds true in the language learning classroom. Photographs can engage language learners in talking, thinking, and writing. Using cameras, students collect visual images of the surrounding environment, guided by aspects of the cultural environment they are studying. Then they talk with each other in English about these photos to understand aspects of their own culture. This student-centered photography project provides a framework for students to interact while guiding their learning experience. It also provides them with structure and security that encourage self-confidence and motivation, the keystones of learning.

With photography as the catalyst, and in ways eminently suitable for mixed-ability classrooms, the student project described in this chapter investigates how visual strategies can help students study cultural beliefs about the natural environment at the same time as learning English as a foreign language. There is a long tradition of using photography and film to document aspects of culture and society (Coles, 1997). One source particularly worthy of mention is *Visual Anthropology: Photography as a Research Method* (Collier & Collier, 1986), which covers practical subjects such as construction of shooting guides as well as underlying principles of visual research interpretation.

This photography project is used in a semester-long course on sociology of the environment and introduces students to the idea that culture may predispose people to certain views of the natural environment and the place of humans within it. It illustrates how language learning, sociology, and photography can be combined in the design and delivery of a course with active and cooperative dimensions. In general, our approach can provide one model for developing visual projects in any content-based course that is designed in whole or in part around active and cooperative learning (Bassano & Christison, 1995).

CONTEXT

This project was conducted in English at Miyazaki International College, in Japan. The mission of this small experimental college is to integrate language (English) and content (sociology) learning and teaching. A language specialist and a content specialist collaborate in the design of classroom activities and share team teaching responsibilities. Using a process of action, observation, reflection, and planning, these teaching partners developed the photography project. Designed for use with a multilevel population, step-by-step tasks guide students through content using active and cooperative modes of learning (Bassano & Christison, 1995). In a sense, this project serves as a microcosm or test case for sustained content-based learning and teaching (SCBLT). In SCBLT, if language is the vehicle and content drives the language, then how students learn is as important as what they learn (Murphy & Stoller, 2001). These assumptions undergird this chapter.

In any English language classroom, each student's level of understanding and ability is different, no matter how accurate or effective the initial assessment and placement of students. Multiple levels of understanding can be defined by many factors that describe differences in how students learn. However, the most relevant factors that distinguish one student from another are individual language ability and, most important, how much each student decides to invest in the learning process. Thus, it is no surprise that the Japanese students in our classroom were not homogenous—their English abilities ranged from beginning to high-intermediate levels of proficiency, with different areas of strength and weakness. These students were in their first year of college and had studied English for 4–6 years in secondary school. In 1st-year academic courses, one of the primary goals is to develop students' confidence in speaking so that they become comfortable actually using the English they have already learned (as a school subject) to communicate. No matter what level or ability, developing individual accountability for what they are learning is critical to this approach—thus, our commitment to active and cooperative modes of teaching and learning.

Active language learning involves students in a process of learning that goes beyond just listening. They cannot remain passive listeners; they must become involved in their own learning in order to apply what they are learning in some way (Meyers & Jones, 1993). Cooperative learning strategies enhance active learning because the use of these strategies requires students to do things and think about things that they are doing together as a group (Bassano & Christison, 1995). Learning to work as a team is often seen as the most important context in which active learning is carried out. Working as a team on structured tasks engages students in a meaningful way and motivates and encourages them to try to use the target language.

Active learning does not appear out of thin air, however, so teachers must provide students with content that guides them through specific tasks, defines roles, and sets forth final goals. This learning framework is based on two important aspects: students studying specific content for an extended time in a second language and learning the language they need in order to do this (Murphy & Stoller, 2001; Pally, 2000). The general content objective of the course is to enhance students' understanding of culture and the relationship between culture and the natural environment, especially in Japan. In terms of language instruction, the goal is to use the language for specific purposes and build on students' knowledge and experience. Therefore, "the achievement of content objectives is considered necessary and sufficient evidence that language learning objectives have been achieved" (J. C. Richards & Rodgers, 2001, p. 211). Moreover, SCBLT, like so many theories with roots in the communicative approach, makes two major shifts: from mastery of structures to communicative proficiency in specific areas and from simply learning language to using language to learn.

CURRICULUM, TASKS, MATERIALS

Stage 1: Concept

The first stage in designing this activity was to identify a relevant conceptual orientation that might lend itself to depiction with photographs. Further, because one of our overall content goals was to introduce students to the idea of comparing cultures, we looked for a conceptual framework that would facilitate this. One such framework is that of Kluckhohn and Strodtbeck (1961), as elaborated by Stewart and Bennett (1991). After reviewing the relationship between humans and nature in many different cultures, Kluckhohn and Strodtbeck isolated three general assumptions about the natural world that may be dominant in any culture. One is that humans can and should control nature, a view that may dominate the cultural mainstream in societies such as the United States. This may sometimes take the form of abusing or harming the natural world. A second view is that nature and people should exist in essential harmony, that is, humans are an integral part of nature. This has traditionally been thought to characterize many people in Asian societies, including Japan. Finally, in some cultures, such as the Columbian Mestizo culture, people may lean toward the view that humans are helpless in the face of nature's power. Any culture, of course, has individuals representing all of these views, but the theory is that there is a preponderance of belief in one direction or another. In addition, we take the view that one must be cautious about generalizing about any aspect of culture, inasmuch as there is complexity and diversity in any society. In practice, after setting up the theoretical framework, we look for ways to point out these important caveats to students as the project unfolds.

Having chosen a conceptual orientation, we introduce it to students by using photographs of representative environments. Thus, a photograph of destruction to a coastal area caused by a tsunami or hurricane was shown and the power of nature was discussed. Then a picture of a large dam was used to illustrate humans controlling nature. Finally, an image of a Shinto shrine in a cedar forest represented the "harmony with nature" view. Groups of students were asked to look at the three photographs and write down two or three characteristics that might distinguish one environment from the others in order to work toward a working definition of each of the three orientations. The concepts are then formally introduced, and students classify the photographs accordingly. Additional photos are handed out, and again the groups work together to identify which orientation each is intended to exemplify.

At this stage, there is also an introduction to the use of photography in sociology, which helps students develop the cognitive academic language needed to describe these ideas and their relationships. The information provided by each photograph provides visual support to help students grasp the content and organize their ideas (Mohan, 1986). This prepares students for the language demands of this project. During these tasks, students of varying levels must listen to each other and share their ideas. This type of structured, meaningful interaction develops interdependence and is a crucial factor in learning how to learn and a key to success in the mixed-ability classroom.

Stage 2: Preparation

In preparation for fieldwork, we provide guidelines that include a map of the area, photo topics, and a photo log (see the Appendix for the main assignment). The first step is to familiarize students with the area, so we try to group students who are more familiar with the neighborhood with others who commute to school. The next step is to go over the photo topics along with basic elements of photography, such as framing and lighting. This is illustrated using the photographs we selected for Stage 1. Finally, while collecting images during fieldwork, students fill out a photo log—a simple three-column record indicating every picture's view, description, or content and the orientation to nature that is represented. To illustrate each of these tasks, the photographs from Stage 1 are used, providing further opportunities to discuss known materials from fresh angles.

Stage 3: Fieldwork

The experiential component in this project is another important element of active learning. Students go into the field and collect photographs as a way of demonstrating their understanding of the three conceptual orientations that people or cultures might have toward nature. They work in pairs to do this, which allows students to learn from each other and teach each other by sharing their perspectives on the concepts and potential photographs. Each student does, however, take his or her own 12 photos. (When we first started this project, we used disposable cameras, but now all our students have cell phones that can take digital pictures.)

An entire 3-hour class session is used for this part of the project, which provides structure in the sense of having all students complete the activity at the same time. Located in an urban area, the environment within walking distance of the campus includes a river, a bottling plant, areas of traffic congestion, dams and water-level control devices, bamboo groves, rice farms and paddies, forested areas, evidence of recent typhoon damage, and hillsides that are protected from mudslides with various concrete restraints. Using small paved roads, farmers' trails, and sidewalks, students are able to circumnavigate the area around the college in less than 3 hours (a distance of about 1.5 kilometers, or .93 mile), even taking into consideration the time they need to take photographs. Within this context, students are self-directed, share what they are learning, and seem to have no trouble coming up with images. This part of the process provides still more opportunities for interaction in the target language among students at different levels of ability.

Stage 4: Work With Photos

Following their fieldwork, students have their photos printed and bring them to the next class session. They review the information in their photo logs, and on the back of each image write the orientation to nature that it represents. Finally, they sort their photos into three groups according to the three concepts (see Figure 1).

Next, each group member looks through the three groups of photos and chooses one photograph that best represents each of the three orientations to

Figure 1. Students Collaboratively Sort Photos According to Cultural Concepts

nature. After they choose their three best photos, they add several keywords to each picture to help them describe and explain their photos to the others in the group.

The subsequent discussion task is for group members to present their best photos and explain why each illustrates one of the three concepts. Students are encouraged to help one another by asking for clarifications and offering fur ther interpretations of the photos. The group then selects one photo that best illustrates each of the three orientations toward nature, and they mount them on a small poster along with keywords and phrases. Each group prepares three small posters representing the three orientations to nature and, with the help of a teacher-provided model and a planning worksheet that includes a list of spe cialized vocabulary, practices presenting the information within the group (see Figure 2). The guidelines for the presentation are to begin with a general intro duction of the location and orientation, follow up with a more detailed explana tion, and conclude with a review of the most important points (Harrington & LeBeau, 1996).

Visual representations, in this case photographs and posters, can be a keystone in communicative language development, especially fluency. We describe students' photographs as "cultural texts" because they help students bring concepts into focus by framing their visualization (See, 2000). After students have studied each photograph, they choose keywords and short phrases to help them organize and remember ideas and important vocabulary. Relying on visual clues and keywords for support, learners are given the security that is needed to use the language with confidence. The posters are also significant for boosting listeners' comprehension by offering concrete visual reference points and vocabulary. This gives students with varying proficiency levels the support they need to ask a question or initiate a conversation in response to presentations.

Motivation is the most important factor. The more students are interested in the activity, the more they feel the desire to communicate in the target language. That is to say, they understand what they want to say in their first language, and this intrinsic motivation encourages them to try to express it in the target language.

In Stage 4, students have numerous opportunities to talk about their work and ideas and to listen to others do the same. They participate in discussions concern ing the selection of the best photos, an activity that involves making intellectual and aesthetic judgments, defending opinions, and negotiating consensus. They also create small posters that support their language needs and practice presenting the main information within groups, giving group members chances to support and help one another improve. Ideally, in doing all of this, they further their awareness that collaborative learning works effectively, and perhaps their use of collaborative skills even becomes a central learning strategy that can be used in other times and places. Underlying the development of collaborative skills is the notion that everyone has different ideas, and in order to learn from and with

Figure 2. Students Discussing Posters Prior to Developing Presentations

diversity, one must listen actively instead of assume. All of these ideas are essential to students' success in a multilevel language classroom.

Stage 5: Reflection and Writing

In this fifth and final stage of the project, three stations are created around the classroom, one for each of the three orientations to nature. New small groups are formed, with each including one member of the original groups. These groups rotate around the classroom in a kind of carousel format, with students describing and explaining to their new groups the photos chosen by their original groups (see Figure 3). Students are encouraged to ask questions in order to understand the information presented. This is not so much a formal presentation as an informal group conversation.

Figure 3. Students Speaking and Listening in Carousel Fashion

Following the conversation, the main information is presented again while students take notes to help them write an essay. This is the final step in the project—a longer paper that combines students' notes and their own opinions and responses concerning which of the three orientations they see more often manifested in their own lives and which they feel should predominate in their culture. This essay is written according to a typical process-writing sequence that includes content suggestions, reminders about devices such as thesis statements and transitions, teacher conferencing, self-review checklists (based on personal error lists from previous writing assignments), and peer editing (see Figure 4).

REFLECTIONS

This project works well at all stages in that students are involved, working steadily (both in the field and in the classroom), and producing good essays at the end. The success is due in part to the fact that the project is low risk in the terms suggested by Bonwell and Eison (1991). It is highly structured, sequential, and carefully planned; made relatively concrete through the use of photography and photo logs; is not especially controversial; and uses a format (photography) with which students are familiar. It also involves considerable instructor–student interaction.

We also find that students' work with photographs—and the resulting

Figure 4. Students Begin Work on the Culminating Paper While the Teacher Circulates

products, both written and visual—are of generally good quality. Furthermore, discussions during the activities produce questions that the instructor can use as springboards for minilectures or to stimulate further reading on various aspects of culture and the environment.

With analysis and reflection, eight reasons for the effectiveness of this project suggest themselves:

1. The entire process is grounded in students' visual explorations of the surrounding environment, which gives the project personal meaning that engages students as they work with images of their own context.

2. Photographs, or visual images generally, engage the emotions as well as the intellect. People often have a more complete response to visual images. They like, dislike, or are indifferent to images at the same time that they have thoughts and feelings stimulated by them. It is possible that this characteristic of visual images is one of the reasons that this project so stimulates student interest.

3. There is an immediate and concrete referent—the visual image—for whatever concept is being explored through language. Perhaps this is especially important for keeping 1st- and 2nd-year students engaged with abstract concepts.

4. The activity is very hands-on, so no one's attention wanders while the work is being carried out.

5. The collaborative aspect of the activity is rich in interaction that prompts thinking about the concepts being explored. Decisions made within the groups affect the final product of both group and individual learning. Students are thus more self-directed in their learning. Additionally, this decision making involves self expression and students have the opportu nity to help one another with this.

6. The activity provides numerous opportunities to teach and learn the idea that cultures, including systems of belief and actual behavior, are intimately intertwined with the natural environments in which people find themselves. Students seem to enjoy becoming more fluent in their discussion of this important dimension of human experience.

7. This activity seems especially well suited for students who are learning English (or any additional language) simultaneously with content, because these students often know more than they can express in the language they are learning. Photographs allow them to expand their expression of their understandings of concepts. Photographs also provide great stimuli for conversational exchanges and incentives to use resources such as dictionaries to look up new terms in order to express ideas.

8. As a result of this project, students become more aware of their environment and of some of the cultural messages embedded in their views of it. In course evaluations, learners report this new awareness in positive terms.

Although this project involves one conceptual framework in one type of content course, the format could easily be adapted to other concepts and courses. It could also be less structured, with the degree of structure depending on instructor and student goals, backgrounds, and readiness for higher risk. The basic elements of the project would remain the same:

- conceptual content (theoretical framework)
- photography or visual assignment
- collaborative classroom work or fieldwork
- posters or some means of display and presentation
- relevant speaking and writing activities

An example of using different content learning with the same approach comes from our 1st-year Economics and Environmental Issues course. One project involves collecting photos from the Miyazaki Museum of Natural History from three time eras: primitive, premodern, and modern. These are incorporated into a study of economics and the environment among societies at different levels of development. In another example, from general English course projects, students are assigned to visit the zoo or another interesting place, collect photos of a specific activity or exhibit, and interview an associated staff member or worker. A third example, from another sociology course, involves a curriculum unit on selfhood or identity. Students create 12 images in response to the question "Who am I?"; sort them into social roles, personal views, and other categories; make posters; and present themselves to one another, first in speaking and then in writing.

With reference to the last example, it is worth noting that it is similar to the approach taken by Wendy Ewald in her work using photography to teach English to children in various socioeconomic and cultural settings (Ewald & Lightfoot, 2001). Ewald and others teach this use of photography in a program called "Literacy Through Photography" at the Center for Documentary Studies at Duke University. In addition to self-portraits as a theme for photography and writing, children also explore dreams as well as family and community as themes for making and writing about visual images. The basic features are the same as in our case, namely, placing cameras in the hands of active learners and using the resulting pictures as springboards for self-expression and the sharing of knowledge through written and spoken language.

We feel that these basic elements of photography, conceptual content, and language learning scaffolding, in a context of active and collaborative learning, can create a powerful mechanism for engaging students in ways that facilitate learning of both content and language. Furthermore, all of this takes place in ways that effectively enable and empower multilevel or mixed-ability groups of students.

Walter Gene Pleisch teaches in the interdisciplinary content-based instructional program at Miyazaki International College, a Japanese liberal arts college where content courses are team-taught in English and the principles of sustained content-based language teaching and learning are applied. He is interested in student-centered discourse that develops listening skills.

Joel See is a professor of sociology and anthropology at the University of New England, in Maine, in the United States. On leave from 2000 to 2002, he taught at Miyazaki International College, in Japan. He teaches environmental sociology, visual sociology, and cultural anthropology, and he often incorporates photography into his classrooms.

APPENDIX: PHOTOGRAPHING THE NATURAL ENVIRONMENT

Please take 12 photos in the natural environment surrounding our campus.

Please take photos of the following scenes:

1.a. Human beings trying to control nature (3 photos)

> CONTROL = to have power or authority over something
> To control nature means to try to have power over nature.

1.b. Human beings abusing nature (3 photos)

> ABUSE = to hurt badly
> To abuse nature is to hurt the natural environment.

2. The power of nature (3 photos)

> POWER = strength or ability to do something
> Nature has strength or power that humans must deal with.

3. Humans and nature in harmony (3 photos)

> HARMONY = peaceful cooperation
> We can see harmony or peaceful cooperation in the natural environment.

iDeas for iPods in the Multilevel Language Classroom

Troy Cox, Robb Mark McCollum, and Benjamin L. McMurry

It is the first day of school. You walk into your classroom and see some students talking, others looking through papers, and a few listening to music on distinctive white headphones. You have everyone get ready so you can start class. As the students introduce themselves, you realize their speaking abilities are quite mixed. You want to test their writing, so you take them to the computer lab to have them type an essay. While there, you realize that although they like using technology, some are having trouble even locating the word-processing software, while others are skillfully using a thesaurus via your school's online library access.

You start thinking about how you can use students' interest in technology to address the challenge of their mixed ability levels, and you realize that one way would be to engage in project-based learning using iPods and other MP3 players that some of the students already have (Mathews-Aydinli & Van Horne, 2006). By having students of varying language proficiencies and levels of technological expertise work together, meaningful communication can occur for students at all ability levels.

CONTEXT

Our recommendations for using iPods in the language classroom are based on our experience teaching at an intensive English program in the western United States. The majority of learners in our program are preparing for entrance into an English-medium university. Each semester our program serves roughly 250–300 students from numerous cultural, linguistic, and socioeconomic backgrounds. This variation frequently results in a multilevel classroom mixture in terms of linguistic and technological skills. Although students in our program are placed in a level based on overall English proficiency, they tend to vary greatly in terms of their individual language strengths and relative degree of computer knowledge and experience. In this context, group work is beneficial not only for the communicative benefits that interaction brings to language learning, but also for the opportunity it gives students to complement each other's strengths and teach and learn from one another.

CURRICULUM, TASKS, MATERIALS

What is an iPod? This question is not as simple as it seems. Apple introduced the iPod in 2001, and since that time at least 30 different models or configurations of iPods, as well as a variety of other similar digital music devices, have entered the market. We suggest that all iPods include the following common features:

- disk storage (hard drive or flash memory)
- control interface (e.g., click wheel, touch wheel, touch screen)
- logic board
- audio jack
- battery
- user interface

With the exception of the Shuffle models, all iPods also have a screen, which provides user access to menu-ordered selections. Please note that as we discuss iPods in this chapter, we are referring to models with a screen or display. In addition, although we use the term *iPod* because it is far and away the most common of such devices (Cruz, 2007), other MP3 players and comparable products could also be used. Because an iPod is in essence a simple computer, it can be programmed to do a variety of tasks, and a number of accessories have been created that work in tandem with it. Not all models, however, are compatible with the accessories that are on the market. As technology evolves, it is important to verify compatibility.

There are many activities that are fun and easy to implement using iPods in a multilevel English language classroom. Our chapter is meant as an overview, not a comprehensive list, and it is our hope that some of our ideas will spark creative new ideas for your context.

Audio Activities

The iPod can be used for more than just listening to music. Podcasts (discussed in more detail later in the chapter) are widely available and include a huge variety of audio segments and programs that can be used in the classroom. Diverse content that is available online includes university lectures, movie reviews, consumer product reviews, audiobooks, political commentaries, comedy, advertisements, instructions for how to do given tasks, religious sermons, therapeutic advice, and countless others. (Web sites with potential content are nearly endless, but one might begin searching, for example, in the iTunes U section of the iTunes Store.)

Connecting an iPod to speakers via the headphone jack allows all class members to listen to the same segment—just as with a traditional cassette or CD player. But the advantage is that a roomful of iPods, for far less expense than a listening lab, allows a mixed-ability group of students to listen to different programs that are suitable for their different proficiency levels. Other advantages of iPods include their portability, easy navigability (searching, scanning, pausing, bookmarking, etc.), and easy availability of (often free) authentic content.

Consider the following example: If a class has been practicing giving descriptions, the instructor might decide to use humpback whales as content and to develop listening skills that are relevant to understanding descriptions. One quick Internet search later, that instructor is downloading a podcast on the topic from a university Web site or even a relevant video from National Geographic. During the listening exercise, the instructor could easily pause the recording and ask questions. Additionally, the previous day's lecture on ocean life could easily be replayed to remind students of a point they already learned. Then the instructor could return to the current listening passage and start at the same point—all without switching tapes or CDs and with no rewinding or fast forwarding required.

Another example is that of giving and following directions. Many universities now provide audio tours via iPods or cell phones. If such a tour has not yet been created for your campus, you might record one yourself, using an iPod as a digital voice recorder (see the Digital Voice Recording section of this chapter). Recording the directions while physically doing the tour yourself typically allows for the inclusion of much more specific details. Such a recording could easily be made available for download from a university Web site or classroom computer. Because each student could listen and do the tour individually, those with lower English proficiency levels could go more slowly and listen multiple times, as needed. An added benefit of such an activity is that students might also learn information and skills to help them in their studies (for instance, the tour could include information on how to find books in the library).

Video Activities

All current iPods (except Shuffle models, as mentioned earlier) and many other digital players come with video capabilities. As with audio, a wide variety of (mostly free) authentic video content is available, including science and nature segments, news and sports broadcasts, television commercials, movie trailers, Microsoft PowerPoint presentations, music videos, and the incredible variety of content available on sites such as *YouTube* (YouTube, 2009) and *Google Video* (Google, 2009).

As with audio, video can be shared with an entire class by using a connector cable that runs from the iPod dock to a television or multimedia projector. Once again, bookmarks can make it convenient to switch among video segments. In relation to the previous example on ocean life, it would even be possible to switch from audio to video and back again. Part of the listening could be done together as a class, and the rest assigned as homework. In that way, students of varying proficiency levels could use iPods to develop their listening skills at their own pace and in their own way.

Text Activities

Even older iPods come with a feature to display text. Text files can be added from your computer, and the possibilities are nearly endless: short stories, personal essays, music lyrics, audio or video transcripts, how-to instructions, newspaper and magazine articles, jokes and riddles, recipes, advertisements, blogs, and so on.

It is possible to provide students with texts to use in an information gap activity or a short reading passage to support another activity; for example, students might read along with an audio segment or do a fill-in-the-blank exercise while watching a music video. Although such activities could be done with older or no technology, iPods provide students with the freedom to pause and navigate through the program in ways that are conducive to learning at their specific level of proficiency. Perhaps one student does not understand a word in a song, whereas the rest of class has no trouble identifying the meaning. Rather than holding up the lesson to answer one student's question, or moving on and leaving that student confused, iPods allow everyone to move ahead at their own pace. That student could pause the music, consult the text, ask questions, or use a dictionary to solve the linguistic challenge while the other students press ahead. This kind of flexibility makes the iPod a great tool for teachers with mixed-ability classes.

Web Browsing

The iPod Touch (so called because it has a touch screen) and iPhone, as well as other digital media devices, feature wireless connectivity. If a wireless network is available in your school, it is possible to connect to the Internet and browse as part of a classroom lesson. If there are a limited number of iPods, students could take turns looking for information to share with the class, choosing their own audio or video content from a given Web site or doing research in connection with a writing assignment. An iPod is typically less expensive than a traditional computer, less prone to viruses and crashes, and easier to maintain. Fifteen such Web-enabled devices could provide students with Internet access for just one-quarter of the price of 15 computers.

Digital Voice Recording

There are now many accessories to convert an iPod for use as a high-quality digital voice recorder. Other digital media devices come with this feature without the need for additional accessories. This makes it possible to make digital voice recordings of student interviews and presentations, teacher lectures, and on-the-street authentic speech samples, among other possibilities. Because the recording is digital, it can be easily edited with software such as Audacity (2009). The ability to copy and paste segments of the recording, increase the volume of people who speak quietly, and other features makes the use of digital audio much more attractive and flexible than older options. As with other types of audio and video, such recordings can be made available for download through a university Web site or classroom computer.

One activity that can help students gain a greater awareness of their speech, including pronunciation and intonation, is to have them transcribe a recording of themselves or a classmate, perhaps of a brief presentation given in class. Listening to themselves speak English is often an illuminating (or shocking) experience for learners, and it can lead to productive goal setting, practice opportunities, or teacher–student conferences. In a multilevel classroom, this kind of personalized attention is a great way to help each individual improve.

Podcasting

Instead of distributing audio files through a university Web site or classroom computer, these files can also be posted on a Web site that has a Really Simple Syndication (RSS) feed. This in essence creates a podcast to which students can subscribe so that anytime a new audio or video file is posted, it will automatically download to the students' iPods or other devices.

Podcasts are digital files that are disseminated over the Internet. They are similar to radio or television programs, may contain audio or video content, and are available on demand. It is easy to search for, subscribe to, and publish podcasts using software such as Apple's iTunes (2009), available for both Macintosh and Windows computers. There are literally thousands of commercial programs available on topics such as health, recreation, world news, government, hobbies, and more.

Current Issues Project Podcast

Although podcasts provide a rich source of input for students, there is also the possibility of having students create their own. In our classes, we have done what we call a Current Issues Project Podcast (CIPP), which combines the advantages of project work with those of iPod technology to provide effective learning opportunities for students of mixed abilities. The CIPP is an integrated skills project that makes use of the iPod and podcasts for receiving, recording, and sharing student work on a current topic of high interest. Students learn how to join the podcasting community while honing their English listening, speaking, reading, and writing skills. Because this is a group project, it is ideal for multilevel settings and encourages learners to support and assist one another.

CIPP activities include listening to podcasts, conducting interviews using a digital voice recorder, transcribing and summarizing the interviews, and reporting findings via a podcast for digital dissemination to classmates. It is designed for students at high-intermediate to advanced levels but could be easily adapted to meet the needs and objectives of lower level classes as well. We have used this project structure in a midlevel traditional listening-speaking classroom as well as in an upper level content-based instruction classroom.

Step 1: Selecting an Issue

Instructors divide students into project teams, ensuring that each group has a mix of language abilities and technology skills. Once groups are formed, students choose a current issue or problem of interest for study. Some that have been chosen in our classes include abortion, immigration, gun control, and environmental issues. As long as the controversial nature of the topic is not excessively sensitive or threatening, the significant content and high interest can be quite motivational and enhance learning. Instructors might help steer groups away from topics that evoke emotions that are too strong, and they might help identify relevant and level-appropriate audio and video materials. Instructors might also want to limit the project to issues that relate to course themes or objectives.

Step 2: Locating Podcasts

Instructors should introduce and explain the technology of podcasts in simple terms, including showing students how to find ones that are relevant to their chosen topics. Teams can subscribe to a list of such podcasts and download them to their iPods or other devices for convenient listening. Next, they summarize their programs by taking notes and writing summaries. These podcasts are the source material that groups use as a research foundation for their issue or problem.

Step 3: Conducting Interviews

After building such a foundation, teams create a list of interview or survey questions on their topic based on what they learned from the podcasts and other materials. They should plan to interview community members, possibly recording the interviews for later transcription. If digital recording is not possible, students should take notes and write summaries.

Step 4: Reporting Findings

Upon completion of their data collection, students are now ready to develop their findings into a report of their own. Instructors should provide models of how to put such a report together, including references. Teams then develop and present an oral report that summarizes the issue, their findings (from primary as well as secondary sources), and their own responses and recommendations. Software such as Microsoft PowerPoint or OpenOffice.org Impress (2007) might be used to create a slide show to accompany the oral presentation.

Step 5: Creating a Podcast

Students can become digital publishers by converting their oral (and possibly visual) report into a podcast and making it available for download on the Internet. Teams should plan their oral report carefully. We encourage students to prepare a script or detailed outline and practice speaking prior to recording. Depending on the choice of software, creating a podcast can be as easy as hitting the Record button. Groups can also attach video or image content to their podcasts with the help of software such as GarageBand (2009) or Podcast Generator (Betella, 2007). Once the podcast has been polished and saved, the completed project can then be uploaded and put on the Internet as a brand-new podcast.

The CIPP is an integrated skills project that encourages students to make use of current, authentic resources as they learn about and investigate a meaningful issue. Through the use of podcast collection, research interviews and surveys, and report presentation, students in mixed-ability groups exercise and develop their English listening, speaking, reading, and writing skills as they work on an academic content project. Students are motivated to carry out all the work involved due to the opportunity to learn technological skills and create a finished product that is made available to a literally worldwide audience.

REFLECTIONS

As with any technology, the effectiveness of using iPods in language instruction in a mixed-ability setting is dependent on the underlying principles on which the instruction is based. People tend to look at new technology and think of the things that could be done without asking *whether* they should be done. But if the instructional principle is sound, then the likely effectiveness and fruitfulness of an iPod activity increases. The point, after all, is not the technology, but the learning outcomes. The question is not "How might we play with these new toys?" but rather "Will using this technology complement or enhance learning?" Technology should never overshadow language learning objectives. Specifically, instructors might ask questions such as these:

- Will this activity require or benefit from students working individually at their own pace and at their own level?

- Will this activity require or benefit from device portability?

- How long will it take to learn the necessary technology to do this activity? Will it be used more than once during the course?

- How important or motivating are ease of access, up-to-date content, and a digitally published product as part of the means and ends?

When using technology, plenty of practice time is required in order to learn how to use the tools effectively. Teachers need time to master the technology before using it with a class. Then enough time needs to be put into the schedule for students to familiarize themselves with the basics before actual language learning activities begin. Once these issues have been addressed, however, using a new technology can often engage students more fully. Then iPods and similar devices can become powerful tools for collaboration and progress in a mixed-ability language classroom.

Troy Cox is the technology and assessment coordinator at the English Language Center at Brigham Young University, in Provo, Utah, in the United States.

Robb Mark McCollum teaches ESL and TESOL courses for the Center for American English Language and Culture at the University of Virginia, in the United States.

Benjamin L. McMurry is an ESL teacher at the English Language Center at Brigham Young University, in Provo, Utah, in the United States. He is also completing a PhD in instructional psychology and technology.

CHAPTER 9

Teaching Smart, Using Art: Creativity at Work in Mixed-Ability Classes

Linda M. Holden

All learning begins with our five senses—sight, sound, smell, taste, and touch—out of which the arts emerge. The senses are the vanguard through which all data must pass for us to make sense or meaning out of our surroundings and experiences. Because the arts present a natural outflow and expression of the senses, this chapter examines their role and impact in satisfying the wide-ranging needs of students in mixed-ability or multilevel classes.

The arts, whether fine or pop, may be defined as any means of expression that imaginatively activates and stimulates the processing of sensory information. Artistic means or formats include (but are certainly not limited to) painting, photography, drawing, clip art, postcards, cartoons, music—from classical, country, and jazz to the Beatles, karaoke, and movie themes—jazz chants, drama and role-plays, play dough or pipe-cleaner sculptures, coloring pages, sketching, handmade projects, and manipulation of refrigerator magnet words.

Given that all cultures express their distinctiveness and creativity through food, painting, drama, music, sculpture, architecture, and other sensory-based media, the arts proffer remarkably fertile ground for teaching culturally diverse second language learners. Arts-based activities capture and sustain students' interests because they closely parallel cultural and artistic expressions from students' own backgrounds. The arts frame learning ventures within a positive, subjective context into which students of varying language proficiencies can more safely venture, making personally meaningful contributions because they feel more comfortable and are invested in expressing their opinions and ideas.

Coupled with the cross-cultural dynamics of the arts is the physiological factor of right-brain learning and its capacity to assist learners of mixed abilities. Many researchers and practitioners alike consider the right side of the brain to be the storehouse of emotions, memories, impressions, and the imagination. As the arts tap into these repositories of life-based experiences, they activate learners' background schemas, triggering the imagination, ideas, impressions, feelings, or facts needed for expression, possibly via the left side of the brain, generally believed to be responsible for language processing and production. In doing so, the arts help equip learners with ideas, words, feelings, and memories needed for motivation and communicative content within learning tasks. Rucinski Hatch (1996) has this to say on the topic:

> We start contemplating art in the right hemisphere and then walk across the bridge to further process language in the [left] hemisphere. We may speak of left-brain and right-brain cultures. The Western industrialized societies represent a more left-brain orientation. We value technology, science, organization, efficiency, accuracy and proof; while right-brain cultures value art, music, spiritualism, mysticism and mystery. Left-brain cultures tend to value the work of the logical, rational mind; while right-brain cultures value the work of the hands, such as the ability to draw or create a beautiful embroidery.
>
> Although American society is more left-brain oriented, many of our students originate from right-brain societies. Perhaps then it is correct to begin language learning activities in a right-brain orientation where these students feel more comfortable. They experience feelings in the right hemisphere and then are able to transfer these feelings to the left hemisphere where they are processed as spoken and/or written language. What advantage does art bring for the development of language? Perhaps one answer is that the left hemisphere receives opportunities for vocabulary development and manipulation of target language structures. The right hemisphere receives opportunities for use of imagination and exploration and identification of feelings. (¶ 3–4)

Rucinski-Hatch's remarks underscore the potential of the arts for embedding language activities within a more stimulating and productive learning environment.

Adding weight to the cultural and physiological dimensions of language learning through the arts is their social dimension. When real-life communicative acts take place, they transpire between two entities in a social context. Any medium that establishes language practice and expression within a more authentic social context more accurately approaches the environment of real-life communication, thus promoting more genuine social reaction and interaction with the language task and with other learners. Because the arts so commonly mirror real-life stories, dramas, and dilemmas, they can effectively carry the social dimension of communication into learning, thereby lowering students' affective filters while simultaneously promoting more authentic communicative contexts. A further distinctive element of the visual arts is their vibrancy—visuals shine a spotlight on nonverbal dimensions of communication such as body language, facial expressions, and gestures, which are themselves salient aspects of overarching communicative competence.

Because the arts are multisensory in presentation; broad-based in their cultural, physiological, and social contexts; and readily adaptable to pedagogical and linguistic goals, needs, and tasks, they embody a viable and compelling option that supports the unique challenges and widely differing needs of students in multilevel, mixed-ability classes.

CONTEXT

I teach at a community college in an adult education program, where many classes are organized into 3-hour sessions. Students' ages range from 18 to 65. Because the college is fairly close to a large, metropolitan area, our program draws people from all walks of life and many socioeconomic levels. Doctors and engineers often find themselves beside people who have never had the opportunity to finish their education.

Students generally range from intermediate to advanced levels of proficiency and represent myriad cultures, nationalities, and ethnicities from around the world. They enter my classes with an astounding array of educational, cognitive, and experiential backgrounds from which they draw in pursuit of English language competency. During the term in which I wrote this chapter, 78% of my students were Spanish speakers from Mexico and Central and South America, with the remaining 22% originating from Japan, China, the Philippines, Saudi Arabia, and Morocco.

Students' purposes for learning English in this program diverge as widely as their origins but are often employment related. Some desire to improve their English in order to get a raise, promotion, or better job, whereas others aspire to entirely different or brand-new careers. Still others arrive with training and credentials from their native countries but need to master English in order to resume their professional careers in the United States.

CURRICULUM, TASKS, MATERIALS

The Illinois Community College Board mandates a life skills–based curriculum, a framework set forth by the unit topics in our requisite course textbook, *All-Star* (L. Lee & Sherman, 2005). In fall 2009, however, advanced-level teachers began piloting new texts that may not conform quite so rigidly to a life-skills approach. Within this framework, I integrate arts-based activities whenever feasible and advantageous.

It would be far too large an assignment for this chapter to attempt to cover all possible applications of sensory-based activities for language learning purposes, so my discussion here employs as trenchant examples two common art forms: the comic strip and the painting. This section delineates the steps involved in effectively preparing and using these two art forms as launching pads for enjoyable, productive, memorable lessons that optimize long-term language learning gains.

Comic Strip

A high-quality cartoon can serve as a springboard for creating an environment that piques students' interest and builds community, as well as eliciting relaxed, authentic, contextualized conversation (within, of course, the proper boundaries of copyright and fair use). This activity showcases the motivating nature of arts-based language learning as it arouses curiosity, stimulates the imagination, and strengthens student-to-student relationships, all in the process of promoting authentic, dynamic conversations.

To begin, I blank out the cartoon's words in the speech bubbles, compelling students to scrutinize facial expressions, gestures, and body language embedded in the drawings (see Figure 1). Working individually, students speculate on the conversation taking place between characters, writing their ideas in the blank speech bubbles. Then as pairs, students share the dialogues they have invented, discussing and describing how they arrived at their fabricated lines. This always ignites lively deliberation and laughter among students as they compare and contrast their own imagined conversations with those of their classmates.

A short vocabulary lesson highlighting the cartoon's key words and their pronunciation might follow as a prelude to unveiling the original cartoon. When it is displayed, laughter erupts and animated dialogue ensues as students contrast their fabricated versions and those of their friends with the cartoonist's original (see Figure 2). As learners plumb the depths of the cartoon's cultural innuendoes, meanings, and humor, they often make perceptive observations and pose astute questions, leading to more targeted language teaching. When concluding this segment, I often hear "This was so much fun! Can we please do it again?"

This activity readily adapts to other pedagogical settings and purposes because cartoons can be chosen according to their linguistic content and level of difficulty, in accordance with lesson objectives and students' varying needs. I tailor a cartoon to suit intermediate-level students by blanking out only one or two

Calvin and Hobbes © 1986 Bill Watterson. Reprinted by permission of Universal Press Syndicate. All rights reserved.

Figure 1. Cartoon With Blank Speech Bubbles

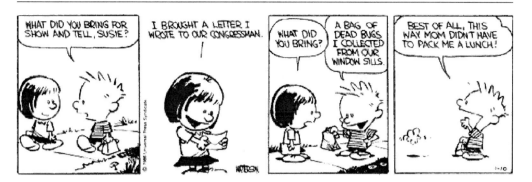

Figure 2. Cartoon With Original Speech Bubbles

speech bubbles, making the task simpler. For advanced-level learners, I choose a longer comic strip with more frames (perhaps from the Sunday newspaper) or one that contains greater syntactic and lexical complexity. This approach to building conversational skills and a learning community accommodates students' differentiated learning styles and mixed proficiency levels, including those of students with learning disabilities. The visual and artistic dimensions help integrate visual, audio, and kinesthetic learning styles within a single task, and the open-ended nature of the activity allows learners of various levels to use whatever language they can summon to complete the activity.

For me, these facts add credibility to the merit and versatility of arts-based activities for language learners. I have used them as a rich resource for practice with pronunciation, suprasegmentals, grammar, vocabulary, idiomatic expressions, phrasal verbs, conversational proficiency, and basic writing skills. Cary (2004) agrees:

> I did some vocabulary and word study work with second graders (capitals and question marks), sixth graders (homophones), high schoolers (informal versus formal register), and graduate students at the University of San Francisco (cohesive ties, prosody, and speech acts). In all the settings, I used comics—the same comics. *Peanuts* had something for everybody. (p. 106)

Variations on this activity include the following:

- Distribute only the first and last panels of the comic strip. Ask students to infer and write the middle section.

- Distribute the comic strip without the beginning or the end. Ask students to invent a conversational start or finish that fits the story. This might segue into a lesson on opening and closing conversational conventions in various social settings.

- Distribute the comic strip, cut into individual panels. Ask students to arrange the panels in proper sequence to make sense of the cartoon and then talk about the meaning of it.

- Ask students to write (and possibly draw) a follow-up episode or conversation for a given comic strip.

Painting

The second activity focuses on Norman Rockwell's *Triumph in Defeat* (as it came to be called—he did not give titles to his paintings; see Figure 3). Students initially engage in an interpretive or response-oriented discussion about it, then move into a vocabulary activity and a discrete-segment pronunciation lesson.

To begin, students engage individually with the painting, noting emotions, impressions, and memories that come to mind while reflecting on it. Then they share these as part of an open-ended small-group conversation. The groups also list all the vocabulary words they can identify in the painting, which I write on the board.

Learners indicate which words on this list are the most challenging to pronounce. As I model pronunciation, students repeat after me. Pairs are allotted ample time to practice particularly difficult words or phonemic combinations. Mingling among the students, I monitor their practice and give appropriate feedback. Learners are now well prepared for phoneme-discrete, minimal-pairs practice targeted at identified phonemic structures that are troubling them. *Triumph in Defeat* elicits such word sets as *shin-chin-skin, smile-tile-file,* and *door-floor-drawer,* among others. I demonstrate the discrete, phonemic distinctions in each set, giving individuals and pairs opportunity for practice. If time permits, students follow up on this practice in small groups by using the vocabulary words to create collaborative stories, which are shared in plenary.

For advanced-level classes, I add a homework assignment wherein students write a personal account of the painting's story. In the next class session, learners post their stories around the room for a "read the walls" activity during which I invite them to envision our classroom as a "museum of the mind." As the learners tour our museum, they read and take in the "paintings" of their classmates' minds through the artistry of their written stories. Students giggle and keenly enjoy this tour while reading and interacting with their classmates' original stories, adding personally encouraging comments to each author's story.

This write-your-own-story venture produces marvelously evocative accounts as students' personalities and perspectives emerge in highly creative ways. Many writers assume that the girl fought a boy at school, concluding that she won because of her victorious grin, despite the fact that she is sitting outside the principal's office with a black eye. In one case, a student wrote that the girl and boy were walking to school on a busy street, the girl far ahead of the boy. He noticed a bus careening around the corner at the intersection just ahead of the

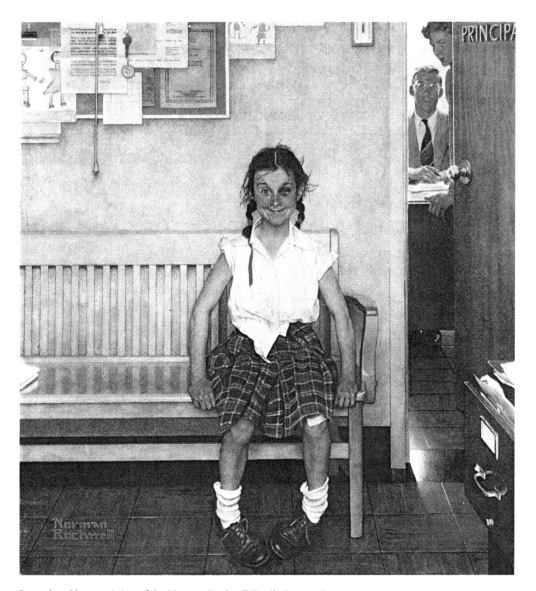

Figure 3. Norman Rockwell's Triumph in Defeat

girl and raced to the rescue, knocking her down and out of harm's way before the bus could hit her. In doing so, he caused her black eye but saved her life. With imaginative students (and they all are), fresh and inspiring versions of the story are always emerging.

   Drawings and paintings can easily be used and adapted for other purposes, lessons, and learners. For example, a different aspect of grammar, such as participial adjectives, might be targeted. This Rockwell painting generates these participial adjectives: *disheveled, wrinkled, pleated,* and *worried.*

On the whole, a painting-based activity such as this one can accomplish three purposes. First, it lowers students' affective filters because they share as much or as little as they are able or feel comfortable doing, with a focus on opinions and impressions, not right or wrong answers. Second, the initial reflective interaction with the painting connects with students' memories of their own experiences, thus activating their background schemas and making them experts as they share. Finally, the arts are subject to personal interpretation, making the open-endedness of the language activities even more meaningful and full of wonderful surprises.

REFLECTIONS

In pondering my observations of students' responses during these and other arts-based activities, I am struck by the power of the arts to touch students' hearts and souls in simple yet provocative ways that infuse learning activities with real-life cultural, social, and emotional meanings. As students identify with that which is awakened within, they are galvanized into expressing what has now become personal. In my experience, this profound longing for communication surpasses that generated by texts alone, literally compelling learners to voice their thoughts and feelings. In this way, the arts invigorate learning activities with liveliness and vitality, affording enriched, enjoyable, creative formats that heighten active participation. These factors—coupled with the adaptability of the arts to visual, audio, and kinesthetic learning styles; multiple skill or proficiency levels; and varying individual needs—make them an exceptional response to the often daunting challenges of teaching students in multilevel, mixed-ability classes.

Some may dispute the efficacy of the arts in language learning, supposing them to be too time consuming or logistically difficult to be practical. Though this may be true for some, this factor becomes easier and options expand as instructors amass a collection of materials over time. In addition, in today's electronic era, it is far easier to find and use pictures, videos, music, podcasts, and other art forms for the classroom with much less time and effort.

Others might claim to find cartoon-based activities objectionable because of their supposedly childish nature. This concern speaks to students' expectations of proper classroom decorum and self-respect. Every student enters the classroom with culturally embedded expectations of what is or is not acceptable in school. But I find that when I explain the role comics can play in helping students understand the target culture and language, they have no qualms accepting them as valid and valuable teaching tools. Still others might say they have no experience with or interest in the arts or are content with their current lesson-designing process, not desiring change. In response, I submit that we as professional language educators must employ every means possible that informs and enhances language teaching in order to pave the best possible road toward innovative teaching and productive learning.

Using arts-based activities, then, is not merely a "nice extra" one might use if so inclined. Rather, the arts can play a vital role in supplying students with the solid substance of which authentic communication is made. This is why I advocate the inventive and selective use of arts-based activities whenever and wherever feasible, for they can arouse interest and participation, engender meaningful communication, reduce anxiety, increase long-term learning gains, and meet multilevel students' needs in remarkable fashion.

Linda M. Holden has taught ESL at the College of Lake County, in Illinois, in the United States, for 23 years. She has also served as an ESL, French, and Spanish specialist tutor and a resource materials writer for the college's Writing Center. She holds degrees in modern languages and linguistics and has traveled extensively internationally, including studying at universities in France and Spain.

APPENDIX: ADDITIONAL RESOURCES

Bassano, S., & Christison, M. A. (1995). *Drawing out: Creative, personalized, whole-language activities for grades five through adult.* Burlingame, CA: Alta.

Christison, M. A., & Bassano, S. (1995). *Purple cows and potato chips: Multi-sensory language acquisition activities.* Burlingame, CA. Alta.

Graham, C. (1978). *Jazz chant fairy tales.* New York: Oxford University Press.

Graham, C. (2003). *Grammar chants.* New York: Oxford University Press.

Hancock, M. (1998). *Singing grammar: Teaching grammar through songs.* New York: Cambridge University Press.

Jensen, E. (2001). *Arts with the brain in mind.* Alexandria, VA: Association for Supervision and Curriculum Development.

McDonald, N. L., & Fisher, D. (2006). *Teaching literacy through the arts.* New York: Guilford Press.

Olsen, J. W.-B. (1984). *Look again pictures for language development and lifeskills.* Burlingame, CA. Alta.

Web Resources

EclipseCrossword: http://www.eclipsecrossword.com/ (free crossword puzzle creation site)

ESL Through Music: http://www.forefrontpublishers.com/eslmusic (lesson plans, an annotated bibliography, and other resources supporting the use of music in ESL classes)

FreeFoto.com: http://www.freefoto.com/ (a source for free searchable photographs)

Fridge Magnet Poetry Boards: http://towerofenglish.com/thepixiepitcoukmagnets .html (online manipulation of refrigerator magnet words)

Picsearch: http://www.picsearch.com/ (one way to search the Internet for images)

Songs for Teaching: http://www.songsforteaching.com/ (includes lyrics, sound clips, and teaching suggestions)

SongLyrics.com: http://www.songlyrics.com/ (contains lyrics for hundreds if not thousands of songs)

YouTube: http://www.youtube.com/ (video clips)

CHAPTER 10

Online Comics: Writing, Reading, and Telling Stories in English

Bill Zimmerman

My love of comics and understanding of their value as a learning tool began when I was a child. Back then, the very best day of the week was Sunday, when my dad would get up early to shop for jelly donuts and bring home an armload of newspapers, all with their glorious color comics sections. The funnies were my paradise—I spent the morning going over each strip, following the adventures of my favorite characters. I looked at the dazzling illustrations and was challenged to decipher what was in the white balloons coming from the characters' mouths or floating above their heads. And with help from my father, I tried my best to sound out the words in the talk balloons and make sense of the stories they told. This, then, is how I first began learning how to read. The comics characters became my friends and family, and I began to realize that reading could be fun and open up new worlds for me.

Through the years, I have never given up my love of comics, and throughout my career as a newspaper editor and author of many books to help people find their writer's voice, I have worked closely with cartoonists to draw in readers to the written words offered in my newspaper and books.

Several years ago, I began teaching English and writing to adult immigrants at the New York Public Library and the College of Mount St. Vincent's Institute for Immigrant Concerns, in New York City. One thing I noticed right away was how comfortable foreign-born students were in using the computer lab to practice their English. Because of their comfort level with technology, and the obvious potential of the Internet to assist with language learning and teaching, an idea grew in my mind. I wanted to create a Web site that would give English to speakers of other languages (ESOL) and basic literacy students an opportunity to create their own comic strips and share their own stories. Using it would be an enjoyable, empowering experience, rather different from typical curricular materials available for such students. Writing and designing comic strips would be an engaging way to strengthen writing, reading, and storytelling skills.

My goal was to build a virtual world where learners would find a variety of well-drawn cartoon characters showing different moods and emotions to choose from, with blank talk and thought balloons that could be filled in with the English words they were learning. These would be their toolkit from which they could construct comic strips that told stories about things that were important to them. The artistic and visual dimensions of the comic strips would stimulate students' imaginations and spark them to express themselves. As McVicker (2007) has written, "teachers can use comics to build strategies to deepen their students' understanding of content using visual literacy skills" (p. 85).

After much planning and programming, in late 2006 I launched a new Web site, *MakeBeliefsComix.com* (Zimmerman, 2006–2009), where people of all ages can create their own comic strips (see Figure 1). This is a free, no-advertising

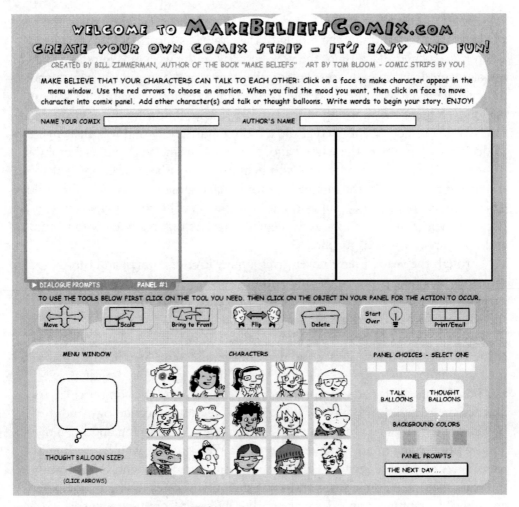

Figure 1. MakeBeliefsComix.com Welcome Screen

educational resource. My goal is simply to encourage educators to experiment with a new tool for teaching language. As a product of the public education system, I wanted to give something back to the teaching community that gave me so much as a young person.

CONTEXT

Telling stories by building comic strips is a way to strengthen struggling students' emerging language skills and make the difficult job of learning English a much more enjoyable experience. Comic strips are a perfect vehicle for learning language. Each strip's two-, three-, or four-panel grid provides a manageable, accessible world in which amusing, quirky characters go about their lives. Readers with limited reading and writing skills are not as overwhelmed in dealing with a comic strip as they can be when confronted with a thick book or a dense reading passage.

Comic strips do not require long sentences or paragraphs to tell a good story. Only a few words are required for the characters to go about their lives and reveal their stories. Anyone who sees a blank speech or thought balloon floating over the head of a character wants immediately to fill it in with words and thoughts—doing so is the first step toward telling a story. Even before designing a comic strip generator, I would take colorful comics from the Sunday newspaper, white out the words in the balloons, copy these now-wordless strips, and ask students to fill in the balloons with their own words and thoughts. Everyone believes they are comedians!

In addition, because computer literacy is an area of emphasis in ESOL and basic literacy programs as a pathway to the job market, the very act of encouraging students to use a computer to create a comic strip provides ways for them to become more comfortable and skilled with technology. As they learn to negotiate a comics generator Web site, arrange and move characters, and compose short texts for talk or thought balloons, they are improving their computer skills and increasing their job market viability.

As one advanced ESOL student from Mexico told me,

> Considering my short experience with computers before and comparing it now, I would certainly accept that creating comics on the Web site has helped me quite a lot. It relaxes me so much by letting me feel free to play with the computer. It is a marvelous strategy that makes me be concise with my sentence writing at the same time that I focus on creativity.

The process of creating a comic strip can often involve collaboration among students, which is not only important in the classroom but mandatory in today's workplace. People need to learn how to work collaboratively in groups in order to exchange ideas and achieve the best solutions to problems. Additionally, the use of computers to create comic strips provides students with focused, gratifying, personal experiences as they manipulate characters and conceive of words that they can type into the templates. A student thus enters her own world, the world of her imagination. Said another student from Mexico, "The comics capture my attention, and suddenly I'm interacting with them. When I see them, I can imagine their voices, feelings, and I think that I can talk with them." One teacher told me that when her students are working in the computer lab and creating their comic stories, it becomes so quiet that she can hear a pin drop, so involved are the students in the writing and composing process. They enter a private, fulfilling world of the imagination.

MakeBeliefsComix.com can be used for a variety of age groups and levels of students, and I offer suggestions for educators (see Figure 2). It can be used, for example, with beginning-level adult ESOL students who want to try to use some of the vocabulary words they are learning in class. With such students, a teacher might create a comic scenario showing what people say to each other when they are meeting for the first time. Online comics also have been used with intermediate- and advanced-level students as ways to practice writing and storytelling, including having the comic characters comment on characters in a book the students have just read in class. Many teachers also use the Web site with younger elementary school students who are learning English or who are involved in basic literacy programs. Educators with family literacy programs have likewise used

Figure 2. MakeBeliefsComix.com Suggestions for Educators

MakeBeliefsComix.com for activities that parents and children can do together as they sit side by side at the computer. Parents and children can collaborate and help each other write stories, which is an enjoyable way both to bond and to learn. Best of all, perhaps, is the fact that creating comics is an open-ended activity, which mixed-ability groups of students can do at their own pace and at their own level. (Additional sites for creating comics online are listed in the Appendix.)

CURRICULUM, TASKS, MATERIALS

How to Use the Site

MakeBeliefsComix.com works this way: Users coming to the site can select from among 15 characters, each having four different moods—happy, sad, angry, and worried. The fact that each character can show different emotions helps spark ideas for stories as the characters interact with one another. For example, place an angry-looking character next to a happy one in a panel, and one begins to wonder what is going on between the two. Why is one angry? Why is the other smiling? What kind of dialogue would cause such a response? The 15 characters are a combination of humans and animals with a whimsical look to them. They are meant to be inclusive and are of various skin colors, ages, and types, including one who is in a wheelchair. All are friendly and engaging so that users will want to play with them and create words to make them talk and think in the blank balloons. There are also story ideas and prompts provided to help students create their graphic stories.

A learner selects a character, clicks on the face that he likes, and that character then appears in the menu window. The user then clicks to choose an emotion, and when he finds the mood he wants, he clicks on the face to move that character into the first panel. He can then add additional characters and talk or thought balloons in the same way. Words are then written in the balloons to convey speech or thought.

Since launching the site in late 2006, I have learned much about users' creativity in taking a template and shaping it according to their particular educational needs. Initially, I had seen the site as a medium to bring parents and children together to create stories and enjoy spending time together. Then, as a teacher, I saw it as useful for teaching English to ESOL and basic literacy students. Soon, I also heard from educational therapists who work with autistic and deaf children and who found the comics to be a way to create scripts for their clients to communicate with them and for their students to express themselves. One teacher who works with students who have Asperger syndrome (on the autism spectrum) says she uses the comics to create scripts to teach students social skills such as how to comport themselves when meeting new people, what to say, and even how to understand people's emotions. Therapists who work with trauma victims have also used the site to enable their clients to voice what is hidden within them. Other teachers use online comics to create storyboards to help students understand complex works that they are reading, such as Shakespeare's *Romeo and Juliet.*

Students reading a book might use the comics generator Web site to extend the story by writing about a character whose life and adventures continue after the book is finished. They might also write a different ending. Better yet, they can use the site to write their own original story. Students might also create a comic strip or series of strips to summarize and show their comprehension of the book's main themes.

Parents and children in family literacy programs can create stories together and then print them out to create comic books or e-mail them to friends and family. Others find the site to be a resource for being creative, calming down, and having fun—something that is desperately needed as ESOL students struggle in class to master a new language and a new culture. Said one student from the Dominican Republic, "Releasing stress and sharing difficult or embarrassing situations that have happened to me or people I know is what I like about using the Web site."

Educators who teach new vocabulary can have students create a comic strip in which the characters use the new words that have been learned that day. One teacher had her students design online comics that included sentences with prepositional phrases. Having to write sentences for characters to speak or think provides an engaging way to practice sentence structure and learn various points of form and grammar.

Group Comics

Recently, I have conducted workshops both for students who are learning ESOL and for students who are struggling to achieve basic literacy. I also began holding training sessions for librarians and teachers at literacy centers and schools that have computer labs, teaching their students how to work the site. This was an amazing experience for me because I worked with students who could barely understand English but who were greatly intrigued by the idea of being able to move characters into a comic strip grid and write words for them to speak and communicate with one another. I thought that because of language problems, such sessions would last for an hour at most because people might get bored or tired, but the opposite always seemed to happen. Some students stayed at their computers for up to 3 hours, sometimes collaborating in teams with others who had higher level communication skills, until they had successfully put together a story and printed it out to show friends and family members. They wanted to show that they could accomplish this activity and tell a creative story.

When demonstrating how to use the site, I generally use a large projection screen hooked up to my computer. Cooperatively with the audience, I create a comic strip that incorporates their ideas and suggestions. Sometimes we first choose an interesting character to learn more about her and begin building a story around her. Other times, we choose a subject, for example, making a date, going for a job interview, deciding what to do this weekend, or choosing where we want to go on vacation. Then they choose characters and call out dialogue for me to insert into the speech and thought balloons. The characters often become surrogates for those of us who are creating the comic. As one student from Egypt put it, "I have such fun when I create a character because it makes me live as another person and imagine what will happen next."

In my view, it is important for teachers to start with a group comic strip and elicit help from the class in choosing characters, scenarios, words, and sentences to fill the talk and thought balloons of the characters. Working together becomes fun, particularly as students begin to see the stories emerge on the page or screen. This helps inspire confidence that they can do this activity on their own, particularly after they see the teacher also struggling to type in the words and navigate the site. In so doing, the teacher reveals that he, too, is learning from the process and that he needs students' help for ideas. Furthermore, the teacher demonstrates that no one, including him, knows everything. We need each other to solve problems.

Starting a group comic, I might ask the participants to choose two characters for the first panel. Then I ask for their suggestions in starting a dialogue in one of the talk balloons. Next, I ask for more dialogue for the other character to speak. Then we try to move the story along to the second panel. Later, when the learners begin their own comic strips, I encourage them to work with a partner to help each other along and gain confidence in their creative skills. I continue to walk around the room from computer to computer to help them along and answer their technological or language questions as best I can.

More Ideas for the Classroom

Making comic strips is an easy, enjoyable way to practice sentence structures, use new vocabulary, engage in make-believe conversations, work individually or collaboratively, tell stories about our lives and the problems we face, and practice creative writing. The animal and human comic characters, in fact, become surrogates for us, and by writing dialogue or thoughts for them, students can use these characters to express what is on their minds or how they are feeling.

Teachers can also create comic strips with their students in which they deal with issues that they know the students are grappling with, such as finding a job, visiting the doctor, or interacting with their child's teacher. It is not difficult to imagine a strip in which one character interviews another for a job, with the two asking and answering typical questions. Doing this in a comic strip is practical and effective, without being as pressurized as a live role-play might be.

Or how about a strip in which a character rehearses seeing a doctor to deal with a physical ailment, such as stomach pain? By creating a comic strip, a student can prepare and practice the needed words and phrases. In one instance, a mother who was worried about her teenage daughter created a strip in which she dealt with the problems her daughter had been encountering at school with regard to other students who harassed and intimidated her. She wanted to practice the language she would need to speak to her daughter's teacher that evening.

Story Prompts

On the Web site, I include many story prompts to give teachers and students writing ideas, including the following:

- Design a strip in which you travel to a mysterious place.
- Design a comic about an event that took place at school today.
- Tell a love story about two people you know.
- Create a strip about your three most important wishes.
- Create a strip that retells a fairy tale or fable.
- Design a comic strip in which a character writes a poem or sings a song to another character.
- Tell a story about the best party or celebration you have ever heard about.

Often it is interesting to give the entire class the same assignment and then compare the different ways students respond to and interact with the topic.

Owning and Sharing the Stories

After completing a comic strip, the student fills in a box giving the strip a title, adds his or her name, and becomes artistic owner of the story he or she created. Students can print out or e-mail copies of the stories they have created, which is a way of validating their hard work. This "publishing" is a very important part of the learning process because students take pride in knowing that they finished and accomplished something worthwhile. The strip represents their efforts to tell a story in their new language and serves as proof that they can cope and create. As one Russian student, who struggled for weeks to complete a single strip, wrote, "What exactly did I learn after 4 weeks of blood, sweat, and tears? I learned how to concentrate and focus better, practice my grammar, be more creative, have more fun by challenging myself."

I encourage students to show and read aloud the stories they have created. They might also color the printed comics and collect them in a portfolio. Some might even choose to create ongoing stories or serialized comics. Entire comic books or classroom anthologies might be created. Learners might also use the comic strip generator to create personalized greeting cards for family and friends.

REFLECTIONS

Throughout my life, I have been involved in many creative endeavors, from running a newspaper to writing books that are used throughout the world by educators and families. But creating *MakeBeliefsComix.com* has been one of the most personally and professionally gratifying experiences in my life. Because so many people are connected to each other on the Internet, it has been relatively easy to get the word out to educators. Teachers in more than 185 countries and upwards of 450,000 people so far have visited *MakeBeliefsComix.com* to create comic strips and practice language and communication skills. From conversations with educators who have attended my workshops and from many e-mail conversations, I have seen the hunger out there for Web-based resources to develop computer and English language proficiency.

The online interaction has also provided a fruitful way for me to gather ideas and suggestions on ways to improve the site. Such feedback is imperative if the site is to grow and evolve. A number of people, for example, have asked for the addition of more characters with more diverse backgrounds as well as for the ability to be able to write in Spanish. I hope in time to be able to offer other languages as well.

One of the shortcomings of the current system is that students cannot easily store in their computers the comic strips that they create. Although more sophisticated users have been able to find ways around this problem, most have not. They can only either print out a copy or e-mail one to themselves. This is a deficiency that I hope to address as the system evolves.

In the future, I would also like to be able to give learners the capability for creating their own original characters. They might build a character by selecting eyes, hair, facial features, and so on. I would also like for them to be able to paint in color the screen images they create (not just the backgrounds, as at present). Some have asked for a variety of scenic backgrounds, such as a beach, a street, or a school scene. Another long-term goal is to find a way for users to be able to animate the characters and even add voices. The dream list grows.

As someone who was raised on the printed words of newspapers and their comics pages, as well as on books, I have learned from the experience of creating this Internet resource that words are also valid when they appear in electronic contexts. Writing is writing, whether on a printed page or a computer screen. There are many ways to encourage writing and creativity, and the Web can be a vital tool to encourage literacy and spark creativity. This project has also demonstrated to me the kindness and generosity of the educational community, which has been so supportive in trying out this resource and sharing it with colleagues.

ACKNOWLEDGMENTS

Special thanks to Tamara Kirson, educator at City College of New York, and her students for testing and using *MakeBeliefsComix.com*.

Bill Zimmerman is a journalist and prize-winning newspaper editor who has many years of experience volunteering with ESOL and basic literacy students. While at Newsday, *he created a series of comic books to teach history and current events to younger readers. He has also written many books to help people find their writing voices, including* Doodles & Daydreams *(Gibbs Smith, 2007).*

APPENDIX: ADDITIONAL RESOURCES

Academic

Cary, S. (2004). *Going graphic: Comics at work in the multilingual classroom.* Portsmouth, NH: Heinemann.

The Comic Book Project. (2001–2008). *The comic book project.* http://comicbookproject.org/index.html

Davis, R. S. (1997). *Comics: A multidimensional teaching aid in integrated skills classes.* http://www.esl-lab.com/research/comics.htm

Liu, J. (2004). Effects of comic strips on L2 learners' reading comprehension. *TESOL Quarterly, 38,* 225–243.

Morrison, T. G., Bryan, G., & Chilcoat, G. W. (2002). Using student-generated comic books in the classroom. *Journal of Adolescent and Adult Literacy, 45,* 758–767.

Ranker, J. (2007). Using comic books as read-alouds: Insights on reading instruction from an English as a second language classroom. *Reading Teacher, 61,* 296–305.

Saraceni, M. (2003). *The language of comics.* London: Routledge.

Schwarz, G. (2006). Expanding literacies through graphic novels. *English Journal, 95*(6), 58–64.

Wright, G., & Sherman, R. (1999). Let's create a comic strip. *Reading Improvement, 36*(2), 66–72.

Comics Generators

Comic Creator: http://www.readwritethink.org/materials/comic/

Comic Life [Computer software]: http://plasq.com/comiclife (This program fulfills similar functions offline, including with the user's own photos.)

Garfield's Comic Creator: http://www.professorgarfield.org/StarSleeper/comiccreator.html

Make Your Own Captain Underpants Comic: http://www.scholastic.com/captainunderpants/comic.htm

Expanding the Boundaries

CHAPTER 11

Culturally Responsive Teaching in a Colorful Classroom

Roby Marlina

Having in one classroom international students with different degrees of fluency in English and with diverse linguistic and cultural backgrounds is a reality in many Australian university classrooms. Sadly, this appears to frustrate some teachers. One day I overheard a conversation between two colleagues. One sighed deeply and said, "I really don't know what I'm going to do with those international students. They're so disengaged. I don't know how to engage them." The other replied, "It's a cultural thing, and mostly their English is just not good enough."

Teaching in a multilevel, multilingual, and multicultural classroom can indeed be challenging. However, when teachers are unsure about how to respond to this challenge, they tend to shift the blame to factors beyond their control, such as students' cultures and language learning backgrounds, rather than reflecting critically on their own pedagogical practices. This chapter argues that teaching English in a multilevel, multilingual, and multicultural university classroom can be less challenging and more rewarding if teachers develop culturally responsive teaching (CRT; Gay, 2000) and actively incorporate students' various diverse social, cultural, and linguistic knowledge into classroom instruction. An activity to illustrate this point is also shared.

Teaching in a multilevel, multilingual, and multicultural classroom includes the central difficulty of ensuring that every student receives an equal opportunity to learn. This is because, as Bell (1991) observes,

> students in this class are very quick to measure their classmates' abilities and to rank them. Beginner level students may feel intimidated by the competition and the more advanced students may feel that they are being held back and become impatient with the beginners. (p. 12)

Although at the university level all students have been required to demonstrate a certain command of English prior to admission, I have noticed that my less proficient students feel uncomfortable or even remain silent during classroom discussions, despite being eager to participate. Many studies have confirmed that students with native-like fluency tend to dominate classroom conversations without realizing that their behavior can limit opportunities for their classmates to participate (see, e.g., Marlina, 2007; Wright & Lander, 2003). The frequency of these students' conversational turns may need to be lessened so that students who are less fluent can be given space to contribute and develop their language skills. For this to happen, Bell (1991) suggests that it is critical for teachers to develop activities that use the same stimulus for the entire class but ask for responses at different levels—for example, asking students to complete a project on a particular topic, but with different questions or tasks set for different students on the basis of their proficiency levels.

In response to the issue of having students from different cultural backgrounds in the same classroom, studies by Edwards (1999) and Muzychenko (2007), among others, highlight the importance of recognizing the influence of students' cultural backgrounds on their learning styles. For example, Muzychenko found that Chinese students learn through watching, thinking, and following rules and instructions, whereas Canadian students learn through doing, risk taking, and following minimal rules and instructions. She further contends that the learning styles of Chinese students are influenced by their cultural values, specifically collectivism, whereas those of Canadian students are influenced by their culture's individualism. University teachers need to consider the relationships between learning styles and cultures when interacting with students so as to maximize everyone's learning opportunities.

The suggestions by Bell (1991), Edwards (1999), and Muzychenko (2007) seem to create additional challenges. Bell's idea would, to a certain extent, provide students at all proficiency levels with an equal chance to participate in learning. But because the idea seems to come from her experiences with community English as a second language classes, it may not be applicable in other contexts. It also requires teachers to generate multiple questions and tasks for a single activity. In addition, her idea would allow less proficient students to participate, but only at their level and with minimal opportunity for improvement or progress. Studies on cultural learning styles (e.g., Edwards, 1999; Muzychenko, 2007) tend to give an impression of homogeneity, that is, that all students from a particular country share the same fixed set of learning styles or that students from different countries must differ from one another in this area (Louie, 2005). Although cultural values undeniably influence students' learning styles, such influences cannot be made into a "user's manual" of one-to-one correspondences between cultural background and effective instructional techniques.

Even if teachers teach according to students' learning styles, there is no guarantee that what is taught makes sense and is socioculturally relevant and engaging. Not all students attend universities with the kind of cultural capital or prior knowledge valued by the White middle class, which is what most knowledge in Western English-speaking educational institutions is built on (Grant & Sleeter, 2007). Thus, teachers need to be aware that "people are competent, they have funds of knowledge (historically accumulated and culturally developed bodies of knowledge and skills essential for individual functioning and well being) that their life experiences have given them" (Gonzalez, Moll, & Amanti, 2005, p. 72). To demonstrate this in classrooms, teachers should develop CRT (Gay, 2000) in which cultural, social, and linguistic knowledge that students bring with them is included in curricular planning and decision making.

CONTEXT

The specific context for this chapter is a course called English as an International Language (EIL), which is offered to 1st-year university students. The course offers a theoretical and practical understanding of the use of English in everyday academic and professional contexts. In addition to focusing on academic writing and oral presentation skills, EIL also examines sociocultural characteristics of English and issues surrounding the spread of English and its development as a global language.

Students taking EIL are usually quite diverse. They are mostly bi- or multilingual speakers with bi- or multicultural backgrounds and have had varying educational and language learning experiences. Naturally, their English proficiency levels also differ widely. Some have completed most of their secondary schooling in Australia or in an English-medium school in their home countries and possess native-like fluency. Some have completed secondary schooling in their home countries and in their first language, have finished a 3-month English for academic purposes (EAP) course, and enroll in EIL to improve their proficiency and learn more about English. In the following section, I share an activity illustrating how CRT is used in this kind of multicultural, multilingual, and multilevel classroom.

CURRICULUM, TASKS, MATERIALS

One of the topics I include in my EIL course is connotation in English language use. The objective is to demonstrate the importance of shared cultural and situational knowledge in order to understand connotative meanings of words and phrases. The topic also invites students to think critically about the differences between the linguistic skills needed to communicate well in Western countries where English is spoken, such as Australia, the United States, and the United Kingdom, and those needed to communicate well in other countries.

One of the main activities I use to accomplish these purposes is called Colorful Connotations. Because I use this activity in a tutorial, I do not explain the term *connotation* or the importance of cultural and situational knowledge and context, because these have already been explained in a lecture. If the theoretical framework is new to students, however, providing prelearning information and tasks would be helpful. The activity runs as follows:

1. The teacher explains the purpose of the task and gives a brief overview of what he or she is going to do. The activity handout is distributed (see Figure 1).

2. The teacher asks students to look at the words for colors in the first column and to fill in the next two columns. The first is what the color signifies in English; the second is an example of the color in a linguistic context. The first color can be done by the teacher as an example.

3. When students have finished, the teacher discusses their ideas with them. It may be necessary to point out that there is sometimes more than one meaning for each color within particular discourse communities, such as religion, politics, or sports. For example, the color red appears in the expressions *in the red* (in debt), *the red zone* (used in U.S. football about the area within 20 yards of the other team's goal line), and *he is a red* (a communist).

Colorful Connotation

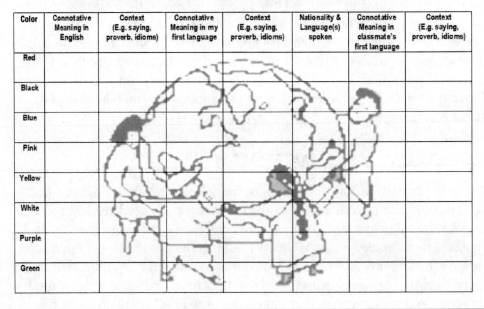

Color	Connotative Meaning in English	Context (E.g. saying, proverb, idioms)	Connotative Meaning in my first language	Context (E.g. saying, proverb, idioms)	Nationality & Language(s) spoken	Connotative Meaning in classmate's first language	Context (E.g. saying, proverb, idioms)
Red							
Black							
Blue							
Pink							
Yellow							
White							
Purple							
Green							

Figure 1. Colorful Connotation Activity

4. The teacher then asks students to think about the meanings of the colors in their mother tongue. Students fill in the next two columns, and their responses are again discussed with the class.

5. Next, the teacher asks students to find classmates who come from different countries and interview them about the meanings of the colors as well as examples of contexts in their mother tongue. They must find a different classmate for each color, filling in the last three columns on the handout as they go.

6. Once students finish this task, the teacher asks them to break into small groups and discuss what they have found. They might choose their top three interesting findings and report them to the whole class. Depending on time and class size, the teacher might also go around the room and ask the meaning of each color from students of different nationalities.

7. The teacher follows up by asking students to explain in more detail the origins or sources of the color connotations in their mother tongue.

8. In small groups, students then discuss this question: "Considering the wide spread of English in the world and its development as an international language, is it important to know the connotative meanings of those colors in languages other than in English? How and why?"

9. Finally, the teacher asks students to report back on what they discussed. Opinions should be shared freely and will involve many of the sociocultural dimensions of language.

REFLECTIONS

When teaching, I try to take into account cultural values and learning styles, but I prefer not to be limited by this perspective. Although it can assist me in better understanding my students, it also encourages me to stereotype them and ignore the diversity and complexity in their ways of participating in learning. For example, if I assume that individualist Australian students can learn with minimal instructions and collectivist Chinese students cannot, I create a deficit perspective that includes unequal attention from the teacher and a simplistic binary opposition between "good" and "bad" students. In fact, who can learn with minimal instructions? Teachers need to be aware of multiple and complex factors influencing the ways in which students learn.

I find CRT effective for a number of reasons. First, it tends to direct the teaching focus toward building students' confidence and self-esteem and making their strengths explicit in class. It allows me to recognize that each student has a unique capability and brings to the classroom impressive knowledge. As Gay (2000) claims, "CRT teaches *to* and *through* the students' personal and cultural strengths, intellectual capabilities, and prior accomplishments" (p. 29). Hence, I utilize the rich resources of students' social, cultural, and linguistic knowledge as a foundation to help them acquire new knowledge and skills. Through this, students feel empowered and more confident and have positive self-esteem. During the activity, I have noticed that those who were less articulate become more outspoken and confident than they were in previous lessons. This is doubtless because they are discussing a topic with which they are familiar and on which they are an expert in the context of the classroom. Those who previously dominated classroom discussions show more eagerness to listen to their classmates. My intention, though, is not necessarily to manipulate class participation, but rather to help all students perceive themselves as having something valuable to contribute and to recognize their classmates as having the same.

Second, CRT seems to provide more room for low-proficiency students to improve. As reflected in the Colorful Connotations activity, and argued by Grant and Sleeter (2007),

> it is important to recognize that all students bring knowledge and linguistic skills to the classroom. If what they know is in a language other than English, then one of the teachers' tasks is to provide an environment in which students can connect new language skills and new knowledge with what they already know. (p. 148)

As compared to other approaches, CRT tends to provide more challenging work and discourage unhealthy language proficiency comparisons among students. Bell (1991) herself argues that measuring and ranking is a problem in a multilevel classroom.

Third, CRT provides students and teachers alike with opportunities to develop their intercultural awareness. The Colorful Connotations activity allows my students and me to see and hear how each color is used in different languages and is interpreted by people from diverse backgrounds. More important, because there is no single correct answer, the task invites multiple interpretations. In fact, my students have found that some of their classmates from the same country had different interpretations of the meanings of the same colors, and some from different countries have discovered shared interpretations. This encourages students and teachers to recognize the diversity that exists within all cultures (Louie, 2005) and to understand that complex and multiple factors affect a person's worldview. Intercultural awareness and cross-cultural communication benefit from the avoidance of stereotypes.

Teaching English in multilevel, multilingual, and multicultural classrooms can indeed be challenging. However, it can also be rewarding if teachers are culturally responsive and work to recognize and activate the funds of knowledge that students bring with them to the classroom. Culturally responsive teachers not only help students gain new knowledge and skills, but also help them build their self-confidence and self-esteem, recognize and respect one another's knowledge and strengths, improve their language proficiency, and develop critical intercultural awareness. To educate students from diverse linguistic and cultural backgrounds, teachers need "to provide them with a sense of dignity in the selves they bring with them into school, and to build on this by demonstrating the social and linguistic and cultural alternatives around them" (Abrahams & Troike, 1972, p. 6).

Roby Marlina teaches in an English as an international language (EIL) program at Monash University, in Australia. He has taught students at secondary and tertiary levels in Indonesia, Vietnam, and Australia. His academic research interests include internationalization of education, EIL, and critical pedagogy.

CHAPTER 12

Unity and Diversity in a Theology Class: Learning English for Academic Reading and Writing

Iris Devadason

For 26 years I taught a course called Advanced English to students of theology who were beginning a bachelor of divinity course at the United Theological College (UTC), in Bangalore, India. This is an ecumenical college in an urban setting, and it is known for its Western academic heritage. From a historical perspective, as too few Westerners know, Indian Christianity traces its heritage from the first century, when it is believed that Thomas, one of the original 12 apostles of Christ, arrived on the western coast of the South Indian peninsula and established the Malankara (now Mar Thoma) Church.

I took over the 9-week course from a teacher who advised me to conduct a diagnostic test on the first day and then send the "good ones" to the library to read novels and write book reviews. They could be left alone. The teacher's main task was to concentrate on helping weaker students who needed more help with their English. Thankfully, I did not feel obliged to follow this advice! Surely, I thought, despite the challenge of a mixed-ability class, all students should be given the opportunity to improve and grow in their language and cognitive abilities. I took a generally humanistic perspective, as exemplified by Ong (1982):

> To say writing is artificial is not to condemn it but to praise it. . . . [I]t is utterly invaluable and indeed essential for the realization of fuller, interior, human potentials . . . [and] interior transformations of consciousness. . . . Writing heightens consciousness. . . . [It] can enrich the human psyche, enlarge the human spirit, intensify its interior life. (pp. 82–83)

Who but an English teacher would introduce these students to the finer pleasures of English as found, for example, in imaginative literature? After all, the

German reformer Martin Luther once said that if theologians did not read literature, theology would fall flat on its face.

The impact of my approach was profound, and the warm camaraderie created by it had far-reaching consequences. For example, female students, studying for love of the subject matter—because at that time (early 1980s) they had no hope of being ordained, and still do not in some churches—were empowered to pursue their studies more confidently. (Though women were a clear minority at UTC, the college was committed to gender equality, a significant stance given that both the Indian church and Indian society in general have a patriarchal bias.) Another example concerns my reluctance to stigmatize "weak" students needing "remedial" education, both pejorative labels with negative connotations (M. Rose, 1983). Instead, those who could benefit from extra instruction were invited to my home for tutorials, which was perceived as a privilege.

This chapter seeks to establish that the underlying goal of an English to speakers of other languages (ESOL) course in a professional college or seminary is to create a unified group or community of learners despite students' heterogeneity, which in my case involved church backgrounds, rural versus urban upbringings, and previous education as well as varying levels of English proficiency. To facilitate such unity, an ESOL teacher needs to show empathy for those from disadvantaged educational backgrounds and take care to cultivate attitudes of inclusivity and even friendship, thus fostering true learning. This is of more importance than questions of teaching methods or materials, which in any case are often based on theories with unfamiliar cultural roots (Canagarajah, 2002).

CONTEXT

The Advanced English students were ages 21–35, mainly young men, and included those from urban settings in which English saw daily use as well as those from rural settings in which English was effectively a foreign language. As a result, many students felt intimidated about their program's requirement for them to be accurate and fluent in both spoken and written English. In the eyes of many faculty members, students' primary academic need was to learn how to write well-organized essays in English. To satisfy UTC's academic requirements, the administration had set up a 6-week, presession remedial course for those who failed the entrance examination as well as the Advanced English course to ensure that every 1st-year student had the proper skills in English to handle dense academic material.

In the Indian subcontinent, where English is a 200-year-old British legacy, the possession of skills in English endows students with power to interact with the multilingual Indian churches and their international counterparts. The needed skills surpass the normal requirements of accuracy and fluency and call for the art of negotiation with imagination and a liberal understanding of human nature. Therefore, students training in theology in a mixed-ability English class in India need to work together from the start of their careers in order to foster a sense of oneness, participation, and peaceful cooperation.

CURRICULUM, TASKS, MATERIALS

Consulting with content area teachers brought out the fact that speed reading and logical writing were important skills required of these students. Because these skills incorporated other skills such as advanced vocabulary and grammar acquisition and précis writing, it was clear that our course should spend time on these areas, so the curriculum and tasks were designed with these aims in mind. The materials used for reading were largely subject-specific and taken from university-prescribed texts. However, I also used poetry and novels to teach critical appreciation and related these to the literary styles in the Psalms, Proverbs, Book of Revelation, and Old Testament narratives.

As is true for many teachers, group work configurations were at the heart of my approach to accommodating various levels of English. Dividing the 12–25 students usually in the course into small groups was an arbitrary process; I did not attempt to balance strong and weak students in each group. Though many resources were provided for lower level students, all language tasks were for all students, and the spontaneous spirit of competition among groups brought out solidarity among those who were otherwise different from one another. This humanistic approach was an ego booster for those who might have otherwise felt isolated.

Cooperative Reading and Summary Writing

Rather than make students struggle with academic English by reading alone and consulting a dictionary for every unknown word, I used techniques to lessen anxiety and frustration. For example, I would assign a book chapter and distribute it to the class, and each group would be responsible for two to three pages. The groups wrote summaries of the text and shared them with the rest of the class. In effect, the whole class was working on discovering the meaning of the text together. Although the task was aimed purely at comprehension, much additional discussion and social interaction took place as well. Regardless of the nature or amount of individual students' contributions, groups learned to cooperate as a team, which to me was the main purpose. Even just listening to others is a useful learning aid for those unused to articulating their views in English.

In class, group leaders took turns presenting the summaries, and other students joined in occasionally to clarify what was being reported. Discussions sometimes became debates as students from different church denominations were stirred to speak according to their beliefs, with me at times serving as moderator. The multiplicity of viewpoints was effectively brought home to the students—and all the while, English was being learned and used. Following this, I asked each student to write a précis of the entire text, at first in 100 words, then in only 50.

Students were quite confident in their ability to do this task because they had comprehended the reading well as a result of group work and class discussion.

Collaborative Vocabulary Learning

To reduce the daunting challenge of acquiring a large vocabulary within a short time (at first one term, later two terms), a workshop approach was used in which six lessons (120 words) from Hardwick (1968, based on a word list by Thorndyke & Lorge, 1944) were chosen by small groups, as with the reading task. They had to provide synonyms, antonyms, and parts of speech for each target word and present this information to the class. Each group was termed a "panel of experts" and sat in front of the class at the teacher's desk to present their findings. They used various dictionaries, thesauruses, and other references representing both British and U.S. English. I did this for more than 20 years, and even students unused to this method invariably responded with enthusiasm. Benefits included group cooperation, confidence in public speaking, and, for the teacher, a back-row perspective on the class's responses to the presentations. I provided additional input as needed; for example, on one occasion I stepped in to explain that the word *primate* meant not only "monkey" but also "archbishop"!

Vocabulary study was always enjoyable and multivocal. The drudgery of learning in isolation in one's room for an examination was eliminated. The oral/aural dimension of saying and hearing the target words in these workshops reinforced mnemonics, and tests were conducted twice each semester to aid and check recall.

Defining Topics and Framing Thesis Statements

Instead of assigning a topic for a composition exercise, I asked the class to propose one. One year, the students suggested the topic of suicide, a social problem both then and now in Bangalore and a subject of pastoral care and concern that revealed an important area of student agreement or consensus. In other years, they wrote on controversial social, personal, moral, and spiritual topics such as abortion, the dowry system, caste, and female infanticide, all of which remain pertinent issues in India today. Other topics chosen throughout the years included drugs, alcoholism, prostitution, rape, child labor, and struggles in the lives of the poor.

Having taught them earlier how to write topic sentences and add opinions to them, I asked students to create a definition of *suicide* and add a personal response. After collecting about a dozen definitions and opinions, the class discussed how to proceed in developing these ideas. The samples on the chalkboard conveyed a range of ideas, so it was a challenge for students to use the ideas coherently in a larger essay or even to select some and reject others. Here are a few examples of what they came up with:

> Suicide is a form of escapism.
>
> The increase in suicides is a reflection of man's indifference to his fellow men.

Suicide is the result of man's arrogance in his technological maturity.

"Am I my brother's keeper?" is the underlying attitude in us all which has led to an alarming increase in suicides today.

This was a good exercise for group brainstorming and reasoning, and it enabled students to practice the idea of paragraph unity. The resulting essays were logical and well organized because a great deal of thought had gone into their composition. If students of mixed abilities had been segregated for this task, there would have been much confusion or repetitive writing among lower level students.

Creating Visuals

In class, I introduced the Reformation using an excellent table from one of the textbooks required in another course, in consultation with the teacher of that course. Once students were familiar with this mode of visually presenting chronological and geographical facts, I asked them, in small groups again, to create a similar chart depicting the Indian independence movement. This called for reading widely and discussing with peers to achieve the goal of producing a final chart created by the entire class. This required teamwork not only within groups but also among groups. Because the independence movement is a topic close to every Indian person's heart, these negotiations and decisions were quite stimulating. Some argued that the movement had started in 1857 with the Indian Mutiny, whereas others preferred the more agreed-upon and well-documented starting point of 1947.

Many biographies and incidents from local history were raised for discussion, and in general the spirit of sharing and learning spread easily across the mixed language levels and abilities in the classroom. Later, I wrote up this specific project in a book for other theological colleges in India, and the accompanying teacher's manual includes one of the best examples of the historical charts produced by students (Devadason, 1997).

REFLECTIONS

Various kinds of formative feedback were given to students throughout the learning process. Summative feedback (that is, the course grade) centered around a final 3-hour examination (Coffin et al., 2003). Overall, course feedback from students was positive. The evaluation sheet covered areas such as the accomplishment of course objectives; the teacher's speed of speaking, audibility, and clarity of presentation; and whether the course was likely to help with future studies, formation of general principles or concepts relative to the subject matter, developing critical thinking skills, overall study methods, and sensitivity and personal growth.

Collaborating with content area teachers was as supportive as was identifying with students' real-life tasks. I was able to help students read at chapel, preach, critique trial sermons, compose prayers and lyrics, translate from first language to second language and vice versa, and make small speeches on public occasions. I strove never to think of my students as "lower level English learners" but rather as future (and now current) leaders of the Church of India and the world.

Iris Devadason holds an MA (India), an MSc in applied linguistics (England), and a PhD (Mysore University, in India) and has taught ESP theology at the United Theological College, Bangalore, South India, for 26 years. She has done pioneer work and published in this exclusive ESP field and has presented at international conferences.

CHAPTER 13

Teaching *With* Students: Effective Instruction in Culturally and Linguistically Diverse Classrooms

Karla Garjaka

> Whatever knowledge we acquire, it is always acquired through language and culture, two interlocked systems considered essential for human interaction and survival. Culture and language are so intricately intertwined that even trained scholars find it impossible to decide where language ends and culture begins, or which one of the two impacts the other the most. (Trueba, 1993, pp. 26–27)

Research, technology, and other factors have led to our current understanding of teaching as a multidimensional action that must be tailored to the uniqueness of every audience. This observation gains in significance when we consider that the demographics of U.S. classrooms have changed markedly in recent decades. Since 1989, the number of non-English-speaking students in the United States has increased by roughly 105%. In 2002, this number stood at 4.7 million—close to 10% of the total student population (K. Miller, 2003). U.S. Census Bureau projections indicate that this growth trend in the non-English-speaking student population will continue. By 2030, school-age children whose first language is not English will comprise 40% of the K–12 population (Kindler, 2002). In addition, teachers of culturally and linguistically diverse (CLD) students are facing challenging new demands. The No Child Left Behind Act requires teachers and administrators to offer to all students, including those who are CLD, equal access to the core curriculum and appropriate support in meeting state and district standards.

Combined, these changes add a major layer of complexity to the already involved task of teaching CLD students. No wonder that many U.S. schools do not seem to be prepared to cope with the challenges. According to the National Center for Education Statistics (1997), only 2.5% of teachers who teach nonnative English speakers hold a degree in either bilingual education or English as a second language (ESL) education. Moreover, most mainstream teachers have little or no training in the differential learning and developmental needs of nonnative English speakers. Among public school teachers across the nation who have CLD students in their classrooms, only 12.5% have had 8 or more hours of professional development specific to the needs of this student population (National Center for Education Statistics, 2002).

To cope with increasingly diverse groups of students, teachers must adapt, reevaluating their roles as educators and developing a more comprehensive teaching style. Teachers need to be prepared to respond to the different levels of abilities, needs, and experiences of this growing segment of the school-age population. Rather than focus on knowledge transfer, teaching must concentrate on helping increase students' self-confidence, encouraging them to take risks, to be curious, and to question. Teaching should help students become better individuals, highly aware of the complexities of the world surrounding them.

To be effective in a CLD classroom, teachers must make a connection between lesson content and students' cultural, cognitive, and educational backgrounds, which are crucial dimensions of the learning process. Skilled teachers are those who are able to create optimal learning conditions for the entire class, not just for a privileged subgroup. They know when and how to provide assistance and how to extend and build on students' cultural practices and experiences.

Starting from this orientation, this chapter discusses what educators should take into consideration when faced with the increasingly common situation of a linguistically, educationally, culturally, and socially diverse classroom. More specifically, it discusses how to create a classroom environment in which learning can flourish and which requires every participant to respect one another.

CONTEXT

Motivation is an imperative factor in the academic success of any student (Dörnyei, 2001). Learners are more likely to be motivated and, hence, to engage in tasks that lead to learning if they perceive not only that their feelings, thoughts, opinions, culture, and knowledge are valued but also the relevance of what is being taught. In other words, teachable moments occur only when teachers invite and welcome students to be an active part of the journey.

Effective teaching starts on the very first day of class and continues throughout the year. To create a safe environment for every student, teachers need to continuously communicate that students are welcome and that they are valued as individuals. The path for doing so starts with constant interaction, so as to make students feel completely comfortable in the classroom. The more comfortable they get, the more opportunities teachers and students have to understand one another, which supports the creation of a learning environment dominated by mutual respect. Figure 1 is one way to visualize the relationship among these factors.

Good teaching does not require teachers to internalize a long list of instructional techniques, though these certainly have their place. And although resources such as textbooks and computers can indeed enhance students' learning, they are not the magic solution. The effectiveness of these and other elements of pedagogy depends on the foundation teachers establish from the beginning. Without creating an environment that is equally inviting for all students to learn, teachers risk alienating part of the class, a difficult if not impossible handicap to overcome.

The secret of effective teaching, then, is recognizing the importance of positive human interactions. Do not fool yourself—there are no shortcuts to take you to the next level of teacher–student relationships. You must walk the entire path to get there. At the end, what differentiates the best teachers from the rest is the way they cultivate relationships inside the classroom. A successful teacher knows that students' cultures and experiences influence how they learn and respond to schooling. Students' different needs, skills, and experiences must be recognized if teachers are to offer an equitable education. This is imperative for true learning to occur.

Speaking to the general context of culturally and linguistically diverse K–12 classrooms, the next section discusses steps teachers might take to foster a learning environment in which respect is given and relationships are central.

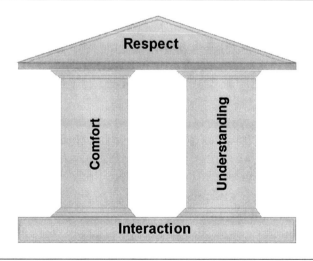

Figure 1. Framework for Successful Teaching

CURRICULUM, TASKS, MATERIALS

Interaction

No education can take place without interpersonal communication. Le Roux (2002) believes that effective teaching can be seen in terms of relating effectively in the classroom. Therefore, teachers should be sensitive to the potentially problematic outcomes of intercultural communication in a culturally diverse classroom. Students from different cultural, social, linguistic, and economic backgrounds may view, interpret, and react differently from teachers' expectations. Teachers must recognize that the more substantial the differences in background between themselves and their students, the more substantial the differences will be in the meanings attached to words and actions.

Classroom interaction inevitably involves forms of linguistic, social, and academic communication. Cazden (2001) points out that the classroom is the only social context where a single individual, the teacher, is in control of everyone's speaking rights. Teachers also determine the following:

- the functions of language, by deciding how it is to be used in academic, personal, and social situations

- the communicative competence of students, by approving or disapproving vocabulary usage, grammar, pronunciation, tone of voice, and other factors

- the cultural communication norms, typically incorporating mainstream language norms from European American ethnic groups and cultures

In other words, teachers have a responsibility to create and foster a classroom environment that supports learning, safety, enjoyment, harmony, fairness, ownership, and responsibility for, to, and from each and every student. Teachers must create a sense of community that is culturally comfortable and authentic for everyone. Sheets (1998, 2005) states that students who relate to other students in socially acceptable ways are usually well liked and included in projects and recreational activities. They are also generally more cooperative, empathetic, and self-confident.

The problem is that teachers and students often misinterpret each other due to cross-cultural conflicts or misunderstandings. Trying to decipher what a student or teacher is truly conveying can be a daunting task, especially when the teacher is not knowledgeable about the "rules" or expectations of communication in the students' culture. Knowing students' cultural styles can help clarify behaviors that might result in miscommunication.

Nonverbal communication is also crucial. This fact makes interaction among teachers and students even more complex. Hall (1959) conducted several studies in nonverbal communication and found that each culture has its own nonverbal system of communication. According to him, nonverbal communication can be classified into categories: *kinesics* (body language), *proxemics* (personal distance), *paralinguistics* (vocal effects that modify speech), *haptics* (communication through touch), and *chronemics* (perceiving and using time). Because the learning process depends heavily on accurate and appropriate interactions, it is imperative for teachers to understand these different ways in which CLD students give and receive nonverbal communication.

Relationships and interactions are essential for understanding and working effectively with different cultural groups, so teachers should make use of various getting-to-know-you activities (such as the one in Figure 2, on the next page). Through such activities, teachers can get to know students better and help prepare them for a rich cultural, linguistic, social, recreational, and academic experience in school. Here are a few other specific tips for professional development and classroom action in this area:

- Research the ways that CLD students in your class make use of verbal and nonverbal communication. This can be done through the Internet, books, friends, parents, and informal talks with students.

- Familiarize your students with rules of communication in the United States. For example, ask students to raise their hands before speaking, talk about acceptable physical distances from peers, tell students to avoid interrupting when someone is talking, and explain that it is not polite to cut in line. Be sure to explain why you are giving them these instructions, because they will not automatically understand.

- Monitor your behavior, attitudes, and style of communication, including your tone of voice, how you approach students, and how you call for their attention.

Comfort

It is not uncommon for people to feel uncomfortable when they have to respond to differences presented by people, events, concepts, perspectives, and values. This happens because we are culturally, socially, and cognitively conditioned to consider diversity to be abnormal. For example, in the United States people are supposed to shake hands when being introduced to someone of the opposite sex, not exchange kisses or hugs as in most Latin American cultures. Also, most people native to the United States would find people in their late 20s living with their parents to be odd, whereas this is not necessarily unusual in more family-oriented cultures. Not surprisingly, CLD students often find themselves unable to display many of the personality traits that are essential to their self-image because of such cultural differences. Teachers should thus be attentive to students' cultural adjustment because this discomfiture can lead to serious academic problems.

We have all seen CLD students feeling out of place on their first day of class, mainly because they bring with them their own cultural expectations and

Purpose: To provide students with an opportunity to learn about hidden rules of U.S. culture and discuss potential similarities and differences with their own cultural backgrounds

Materials: Any movie that exposes students to mainstream U.S. culture (including topics such as U.S. schools, formal and informal introductions, business meetings, parties, sports, holidays, etc.), and a compare-and-contrast Venn diagram such as this:

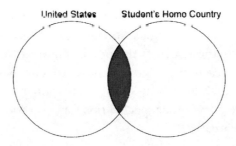

Instructions

- Distribute a chart to each student.
- Play 5–10 minutes of the movie without sound, and ask students to pay attention to actors' body language, movements, facial expressions, and so on.
- Replay. It is important to watch more than once so that students can catch all relevant details.
- Give time for students to fill out the chart. Items unique to U.S. culture go on the left, items unique to the student's home country go on the right, and areas of commonality go in the overlapping area.
- Ask them to share their findings with a partner.
- Open the discussion to the class, and use an overhead projector or poster-size sheets of paper to create country-specific charts for every country represented in the class.
- If students are at an intermediate or advanced level of English proficiency, play the excerpt again with sound and ask them to pay attention to the language used.

Figure 2. Welcome to the United States Activity

understandings of classroom behavior. Having difficulty functioning within the norms and requirements of U.S. schools is a normal part of their process of acculturation. Students go through a period when they realize that their expectations of how things work and how people act do not hold true, which can lead to ordinary behaviors being misinterpreted and quickly resulting in frustration and anger. This happens because our cultural patterns are so deeply ingrained that we only notice them when they are not followed or fulfilled. As Ariza (2006) states, "you can take a person out of his culture, but you may have problems trying to take the culture out of the person" (p. 14).

Sheets (1998, 2005) defines a culturally diverse classroom as a place where students feel emotionally secure; psychologically consistent; and culturally, linguistically, academically, socially, and physically comfortable, as individuals and as members of groups to which they belong. Thus, by offering a comfortable setting, teachers automatically provide students with greater opportunities to learn—

because they are able to maintain cultural integrity while developing ownership and responsibility for their cross-cultural social and academic behaviors.

Although there is no way to eliminate culture shock, it is imperative for teachers to know and recognize its manifestations and to intervene appropriately. Here are specific tips for professional development and classroom action in this area:

- Make your classroom a truly multicultural place. For example, hang flags encompassing all nationalities represented, and post "Welcome and good morning" signs in all languages represented.

- Find a buddy for every CLD student, preferably one from the same country. It is always easier for CLD students to talk to someone who shares their language and cultural background and who is going through (or has already experienced) the same challenges they are facing.

- Talk to students frequently. Do not wait for clear signs of problems to show up (see the activity in Figure 3). Demonstrate genuine care, and help them see you as someone they can count on. All newcomer students will go through a period of culture shock, and you are the person in the best position to help them through it.

Purpose: To provide students with an opportunity to share their feelings about U.S. culture

Materials: YES and NO signs to be posted on opposite sides of the classroom

Instructions

- Place all students in the middle of the classroom.
- Explain that you are going to ask several statements and students are to go to the side that better represents their response. Ask them to be sincere, and remind them that there is no right or wrong answer. Sample statements include the following:

    My school in the United States is very different from the one in my country.

    I like to eat fast food.

    I have a lot of American friends.

    I speak English outside school.

    I prefer to eat my home country's food.

    I like to speak in English.

    My class in the United States is similar to my class in my country.

    I like to live in the United States.

    People here do not know about my country.

    U.S. culture is very different from mine.

- Ask for volunteers who are comfortable explaining their answers. This "why" time is a great opportunity for teachers to notice which students are more comfortable in their classrooms. It is also a great opportunity for students to realize that they are not alone in the adjustment process.

Figure 3. My Comfort Zone Activity

Understanding

To foster intercultural and intracultural awareness and sensitivity, teachers must understand who their students are and to what groups they belong. By doing so, they can help students become aware of cultural differences and similarities. In a multicultural class, students bring to class diverse personal backgrounds, religious beliefs, and day-to-day experiences that guide the way they behave in school. If teachers fail to understand the cultural, intellectual, and other factors that affect students' learning and behavior, it is nearly impossible to help students learn. For this reason, teachers must create a classroom environment that acknowledges, affirms, and respects the differences among individuals and groups.

The North American Indian proverb "Never judge another man until you have walked a mile in his moccasins" is the best way to describe the importance of understanding the cultural backgrounds and experiences of other people. Teachers who are truly multicultural always attempt to view the world empathetically, through their students' cultural lenses. This is why the starting point in a CLD classroom is the teachers themselves. To work effectively in a CLD context, teachers must not only understand and feel comfortable with their own cultural roots, but also be self-aware regarding their own receptiveness to diversity. Teachers will understand their students only when they first understand themselves. They need to develop reflective skills through portfolios, journals, and self-observations, and pursue this kind of professional development throughout their careers.

Teachers and students alike can be encouraged to notice, appreciate, and understand their own and others' physical traits, cultural practices, and language differences, which is crucial for building understanding among all classroom participants. Knowledge of who we are and of the groups we belong to is a complex, multifaceted developmental process that begins at birth and continues throughout life, and it is fundamental for the success of every teaching/learning moment. Cultural habits may indeed guide teachers' approaches to teaching, just as they may guide students' approaches to learning.

Here are two specific tips for professional development and classroom action that can help mitigate misunderstandings and promote cultural understanding:

- Recognize and be conscious of your own cultural positioning and attitudes. The only way to understand your students is to first understand yourself. You might ask yourself questions such as these:
  — What is my own cultural and ethnic heritage?
  — What are my inherited beliefs?
  — What are some characteristics of my cultural behavior that are different from those of other people I have met who do not share the same culture?
  — How do I behave in a classroom? Do I hold any type of prejudicial attitudes or stereotypes that may hinder student learning?

— How do I respond to differences in students' appearances, values, and behaviors?

— Do I view diversity factors such as ethnicity, language, gender, socio-economic status, and sexual orientation as part of the norm? Do I consider them to be as important as other factors such as time, age, grade level, social skills, and academic ability when planning instruction?

• Discuss the differences and similarities in students' cultural backgrounds (physical traits, home traditions, typical day, language, etc.) in the classroom (see the activity in Figure 4).

Respect

Respect is the most difficult value to put into practice in the classroom because it requires the other three factors to be in place already. Hence, to be able to respect diversity, teachers must first become fully aware of their own cultural identities and then investigate the cultural habits of their students through tasks and interactions.

According to the National Board for Professional Teaching Standards (2008), effective teachers need to show respect for diversity and meet the needs of diverse learners. When teachers are not sensitive to individual differences, there can be costs to students, such as lower self-image, frustration, stress, reduced motivation, and increased time spent on specific learning tasks. Although it is widely agreed that teachers' sensitivity to students' differences is an integral part of effective teaching, little research to date has focused on how to develop this sensitivity.

Purpose: To provide students with an opportunity to increase awareness of their cultural backgrounds, to encourage their self-development, and to reflect on and share influences that have shaped their identities

Materials: Blank white paper (one per student); pencils, crayons, markers (two to three per student); magazines (optional) so that students can use pictures to describe who they are

Instructions

• Ask students to take about 30 minutes for this project. They are to write on the topic "I am . . ."

• Leave the task open—they can write a poem, a song, a story, or something else, approaching the task in any way they wish. The only other guideline for the activity is that each line must start with the phrase "I am . . ."

• They may include statements about their hometown, ethnicity, religion, and so on; memories from different times or places in their lives; interests, hobbies, or favorite proverbs; family traditions and customs; or any other topic that helps them define who they are.

• Be sure to let them know that they will be sharing their work with their classmates. One idea is to post students' work around the room and ask them to "tour" and discuss.

Figure 4. Who Am I? Activity

One way that teachers can do so is to stop making judgmental generalizations and start expressing more sensitivity to the depth, variety, and tenaciousness of their own and others' cultures and styles of learning.

An instructive negative example that shows how a teacher, through ignorance or inattention, can disrespect a student is provided by Ariza (2006):

> Mr. Thomas, an eager young teacher from Minnesota, is Caucasian, English speaking, and shows a natural zest for life. He feels great respect and fascination for Native American cultures, and he leaps at the opportunity to begin his teaching career in a reservation school in Oklahoma. He prepares his classroom to look friendly, warm, and intellectually interesting. On the first day of class, he is ready and well prepared for the first lesson. He introduces the concepts he is going to teach with a KWL (what you know, what you want to know, and later, what you learned) chart. He asks Little Flower a comprehension question, and she does not know the answer. In an effort to get a student to answer, he directs the question to another student. The student lowers his eyes and remains silent. Again and again, Mr. Thomas gets the same response from the rest of the class. Mr. Thomas does not understand the mutinous attitude of the class; he is truly baffled by their behavior. (p. 17)

The reason why his Native American students did not answer the question is that they belong to a group-oriented culture. Thus, when a student does not know an answer, the other students will not answer in an attempt to save face or not embarrass the original student. This noncompetitive principle reflects the belief that no one should be singled out because the group as a whole is the most important aspect of identity.

In comparable situations, many teachers find themselves puzzled trying to understand the beliefs, behaviors, and values demonstrated in their classroom by CLD students. Knowing the learning and cultural styles of diverse students can help clarify behaviors that put teachers and students in situations of mutual misunderstanding. Teachers will be able to successfully respect students only when they effectively acknowledge and understand who students are and where they are coming from.

The bottom line is this: Teachers have to constantly and positively interact with students in order to fully respect them. Through these interactions, students will slowly feel more comfortable with their teachers and classmates, leading to increasing opportunities to hear and understand one another. The outcome of this developing rapport is a classroom in which everyone respects and feels respected.

REFLECTIONS

The complexities of teaching in diverse contexts should be acknowledged by today's educators. Sheets (1998, 2005) demonstrates that multicultural education, in its entirety as well as in its component parts, is a multidimensional enterprise that can and must be addressed on different fronts simultaneously. Moreover, due to the fact that teachers are overwhelmed by having to work in diverse classrooms, much work still needs to be done in order to prepare them to truly embrace a multicultural education.

Being cross-culturally competent is a must for all teachers. Even in what is characterized as a monocultural setting, one can find subcultural variations that cannot be ignored. Cross, Strauss, and Fhagen-Smith (1999) describe cross-cultural competence in terms of behaviors, attitudes, and policies that are congruent, converge, and result in effectiveness in cross-cultural situations. Barrera and Kramer (1997) define it as the ability of teachers to respond optimally to all children, understanding the richness as well as the limitations of the sociocultural contexts in which children and families, not to mention teachers, are operating.

I strongly believe that teachers are the single most important resource in any classroom and that they have great potential and responsibility for making every student's schooling experience successful and meaningful. There are, of course, other factors influencing student learning, but teachers' behaviors, attitudes, and beliefs have an irreplaceable impact on students' academic experiences.

The definition of "effective teaching" is broad and complex. Its secret lies in how teachers' and students' behaviors, attitudes, feelings, beliefs, and perceptions are viewed and how they interact. Teachers must integrate students' experiences into the classroom. Only after doing so will teachers be able to effectively leverage other tools and skills, and provide the maximal learning experiences for which students are longing. Effective teachers always prepare lesson plans *with* students, not *to* them, and my hope is that this chapter can help teachers create the vibrant multicultural setting to which we all aspire.

Karla Garjaka began teaching in 1995 in Brazil, where she also served as an ESL/ bilingual administrator in one of the country's largest language schools. Since 2003, she has worked in teacher education and been an ESL/bilingual consultant in the Chicago area, in the United States. She is currently a PhD candidate in educational psychology at National-Louis University.

CHAPTER 14

Minds Working Together: Scaffolding Academic Writing in a Mixed-Ability EFL Class

Le Van Canh and Nguyen Thi Thuy Minh

Teaching mixed-ability classes is a way of life for many if not most English as a second language (ESL) and English as a foreign language (EFL) teachers. S. Richards (1998) has asserted, "Every class we ever teach is mixed-ability" (p. 1). In a similar vein, Rinvolucri (1986) argues, "We do not teach a group, but thirty separate people. Because of this, the problem of mixed abilities in the same room seems absolutely natural, and it is the idea of teaching a unitary lesson that seems odd" (p. 17). In response to such observations, one of the skills teachers should be seeking to develop is that of conceptualizing and employing a specific methodological approach to their mixed-ability classes so that they neither leave struggling students behind nor fail to engage advanced students.

Writing is not only an important form of communication in day-to-day life but also an essential skill for students preparing for university study. At higher levels of education, it is a key aspect of academic literacy that aspiring scholars pursue as part of socialization in their disciplines. Writing for academic purposes is a particularly challenging task for EFL students. The skills involved are highly complex, while at the same time students' cultures have their own norms for structure and rhetoric that are not always compatible with the current conventions of academic English. As Casanave (2002) aptly points out, academic writing poses a "clueless" challenge because the rules of the "game" are almost all implicit (p. 19). Of these, textual competence, or the ability to develop and organize ideas in an academically persuasive manner according to "rules of cohesion and rhetorical organization" (Bachman, 1990, p. 88), constitutes the most formidable and crucial challenge. From our personal experiences as classroom teachers in Vietnam, we agree with Hayashi's (2005) observation that EFL students' writings more often than not end up lacking a clear logical flow and unity, not to mention a persuasive linear argument.

If learning how to produce writing that satisfies academic norms is the problem from a student's perspective, from a teacher's perspective the challenge is to prepare students with varying English proficiencies and from non-English-speaking cultural and academic backgrounds to become flexible writers who can effectively tackle academic writing tasks from a variety of angles. Because students are linguistically of mixed abilities, a particular classroom writing task that is motivating and manageable to some can turn out to be daunting or impossible for others. It is understandable that teachers of multilevel classes often complain that "writing is the most problematic skill to teach in such classes" (Hess, 2001, p. 77). Therefore, academic writing teachers in EFL contexts must cope with at least three difficult questions that emerge in mixed-ability academic writing classes: How can all students get involved in writing tasks? How can stronger students' motivation and interest be sustained while opportunities for weaker students to complete tasks are guaranteed? How can students benefit most from their cooperation in the classroom so that they all can make progress during the course?

In seeking answers to these questions, we drew on a sociocultural view of language learning as a socially constructed process in which collective scaffolding through peer-to-peer and teacher–student collaboration can help students complete writing tasks that are somewhat beyond their current level of competence (Hannafin, Land, & Oliver, 1999; Vygotsky, 1978). A scaffolded approach to teaching academic writing has been adopted by some language educators (Cotterall & Cohen, 2003), but little has been documented about how this approach might be used in a mixed-ability class in an EFL setting.

The concept of *scaffolding*, a term coined by Bruner (1980) and rooted in the work of Vygotsky (1978), has become widespread in discussion of second and foreign language classroom instruction (Cotterall & Cohen, 2003; DelliCarpini, 2006; Gibbons, 2002, 2003; Ko, Schallert, & Walters, 2003). In terms of physical structures, scaffolding is a temporary framework that supports a building during construction. When the structure is sturdy enough to stand on its own, the scaffold is removed (Kim & Kim, 2005). In an educational sense, scaffolding, in the form of coaching or modeling, supports students as they develop new skills or learn new concepts. When students achieve competence, the support is removed and they continue to develop skills or knowledge on their own (Gibbons, 2002). As Donato (1994, cited in Cotterall & Cohen, 2003) explains, "in a social interaction a knowledgeable participant can create, by means of speech, supportive conditions in which the novice can participate in, and extend, current skills and knowledge to higher levels of competence" (p. 158).

Defined in this way, scaffolding is certainly an appropriate instructional strategy for a mixed-ability class where the teacher and the more capable students can create supportive conditions for less capable students through collaborative work. In other words, as an instructional strategy, scaffolding can help create fruitful interactions between teacher and students and between and among students. Ko et al. (2003) expand the meaning of scaffolding by emphasizing the nature of the learner's contribution in any scaffolding situation. They found that "scaffolding is a two-way exchange. For the help actually to work, the less knowledgeable other must be in a position to benefit from what the more knowledgeable other provides" (p. 322).

This chapter reflects on the use of scaffolding as an instructional strategy in teaching academic writing skills to a mixed-ability class in an EFL context. Based on this reflection, it also discusses how different scaffolding techniques can be adapted for students of different proficiency levels.

CONTEXT

This study was conducted within the context of a preuniversity intensive language program in Hanoi, Vietnam. The aim of the program was to enhance learners' general and academic English skills so that at the end of the program they would be able to participate successfully in an international university setting. The intensive English language program comprised three courses: General English (GE) Level 1 was intended for preintermediate learners, GE Level 2 for intermediate learners, and English for academic purposes (EAP) for upper intermediate learners. At the end of each course, a test screened students for the next level. Each course lasted 3 months, with approximately 360 hours of instruction, including 45 hours of writing instruction. EAP students were required to take the International English Language Testing System exam (an alternative to the Test of English as a Foreign Language) and to obtain an overall score of 6.0 for university admission.

The 15 participants in this study were enrolled in GE Level 2 from mid-November 2006 to early March 2007. There were 4 males and 11 females aged 18–20. Although they were enrolled in the intermediate-level class, their actual language proficiency levels, as demonstrated in their classroom writing, varied widely, as did their educational backgrounds and specific academic writing skills.

The intermediate writing class focused on developing students' essay writing skills. By the end of the course, students were expected to be able to produce short essays to explain, discuss, and argue for their ideas. Another objective of the class, though not explicitly spelled out, was to enable learners to become independent, self-aware, and self-motivated writers who could plan, execute, and monitor their own writing and who could enjoy and be willing to take charge of the process.

We cotaught this writing course for 3 hours every week, using the program's textbooks, *College Writing: From Paragraph to Essay* (Zemach, 2003) and *An Introduction to Academic Writing* (Oshima & Hogue, 1997). We also brought in additional materials, which we had developed, to scaffold the learners through difficult writing tasks. The teaching approaches we adopted for this class were process oriented and product oriented in nature. Scaffolding worked in a number of ways depending on the type of instruction being provided, but its inherent

characteristic was support in the form of "simplified language, teacher modeling, visuals and graphics, cooperative learning and hands-on learning" (Ovando,
Collier, & Combs, 2003, p. 345). After students finished the course, they
evaluated their own progress by responding to a 15-item questionnaire covering
important subskills that they needed to acquire in order to become self reliant
writers (see the Appendix).

CURRICULUM, TASKS, MATERIALS

Two major types of scaffolding—teacher–student collaboration and peer-to-peer
collaboration—were employed with this group of students. The former included
modeling, teacher–student conferences, and written feedback. The latter included
peer writing and peer conferencing. Because students had only one 3-hour writing session each week, we chose to use one or two kinds of scaffolding for each
session, depending on the focus of the lesson. In what follows, we describe how
the learners were guided through the process of producing an essay in English
in order to move from being novice writers toward becoming more fluent and
independent writers.

Modeling

Working with models raises learners' awareness of typical rhetorical patterns and
linguistic features of different types of texts. Modeling enables learners to utilize
the new language as a tool in the process of becoming self-regulatory so that their
learning can be extended into what Vygotsky (1978) termed the *zone of proximal
development* (Myles, 2002). As Fower (1994) has pointed out, when students "are
supported by a scaffold of prompts and explanations, by extensive modeling, by
in-process support, and by reflection that connects strategic effort to outcomes"
(pp. 142–143), their writing expertise will be fostered. Modeling activities may
involve discussion and analysis of text structure, context, and language (Hyland,
2003). Figure 1 shows an example of a text-analysis activity that we employed to
teach how to structure an argumentative essay.

For this activity, students worked in groups to discuss the assignment while
the group secretary took notes. These notes were passed on to the group spokesperson to read aloud to the whole class, who then gave comments. Usually, less
proficient students were nominated to take the role of spokesperson in order to
help them gain greater confidence for the subsequent writing task.

Teacher–Student Conferencing

A writing conference is a conversation in which a writer reflects on and talks
about his or her own writing (Penaflorida, 2002). Teacher–student conferences
help the teacher effectively cater to individual needs in a mixed-ability class in
which needs vary greatly. Feedback given in this way also seems to have more
impact because students have a chance to talk about their problems and discuss

In recent years more and more Vietnamese students have chosen to study abroad, partly because more families nowadays can afford to send their children overseas and partly because more grants and scholarships are now available for the students. While studying abroad might have certain disadvantages, it is an attractive option for many people.

Going overseas to study has a number of advantages. To begin with, teaching quality in overseas universities might be better than that in students' home universities. This is often because teachers in overseas universities are more highly qualified and adopt more updated teaching methods. What is more, studying abroad gives students access to facilities such as laboratories and libraries which are not available in their home countries. This certainly helps them a great deal in self-study. Studying abroad also gives students a good chance to learn a new language and new culture. This knowledge might be useful when they come to work in a multilingual and multicultural working environment later in life. Finally, living abroad alone, students will learn how to be independent of their parents, a necessary skill in life.

On the other hand, studying abroad also has some disadvantages. First, students have to leave their family and friends for quite a long period, normally 3–4 years, to complete their studies. Second, studying abroad is almost always more expensive than studying at one's local university. Living in developed countries also costs more than living in Vietnam. Finally, learning in a foreign language is always more difficult and challenging than learning in one's mother tongue, and if students' language skills are not good enough, they will certainly be inhibited when learning in this language.

In conclusion, there might be some disadvantages to going overseas to study; however, I believe these disadvantages are only temporary. In contrast, many of the advantages last students all their lives and make them highly desirable to prospective employers.

Read the model and decide which paragraph deals with each of these points:

1. Develops the argument that the essay defends

2. Includes a thesis that states the side of the argument the essay defends

3. Briefly explains both sides of the argument

4. Refutes counterarguments that opponents might use

5. Restates the essay's position on the issue

6. Identifies the issue that the essay addresses

7. Which words/phrases are used to contrast ideas?

Figure 1. Model Argumentative Essay

solutions with the teacher on a one-to-one basis (Zamel, 1985). Individual conferences might also reveal common problems among learners so that the teacher can offer selected whole-class guidance and support.

In this course, we used teacher–student conferencing flexibly. Sometimes it was combined with written feedback, sometimes we moved around to offer individual support as needed while students were writing, and sometimes we collected common problems and took time out to provide whole-class corrective feedback or to reteach problematic language features. We also offered more extended consultations via sign-up appointments. Prior to such consultations, we asked students to complete a self-reflection guide (see Figure 2, on the next page), which helped them identify specific problems to bring to the teacher–student

Complete these notes about your essay:

The topic of my essay is _____

My purpose in writing this essay is _____ .

My readers are _____

The things I like most about my essay are _____

I like them because _____

The things I would like to change are _____

I would like to change them because _____

I need specific feedback on _____

Figure 2. Self-Reflection Guide

conference. In this way, the conferences were made more relevant to students' needs. Afterward, students revised their writing and resubmitted it for more detailed written feedback from the teacher. If they wished, they could sign up for another consultation to discuss the feedback they received from us.

Written Feedback

Typed comments can serve as another source of support. Teacher feedback can help learners notice the gap between their production and the expected outcomes, point them to worthy sources, and keep them on the right track (Myles, 2002; Williams, 2003). According to Kroll (2001), teacher feedback and assignments are the two most central components of any writing course. Effective teacher feedback therefore reduces students' confusion and frustration (Myles, 2002; Williams, 2003), helping them improve their writing proficiency to the point where they are cognizant of what is expected of them as writers whose work has minimal errors and maximum clarity (Williams, 2003). To help students develop as writers, teacher feedback should focus not only on language problems and ideas, but also on strategies that students may apply to other written works (Ferris, 2004).

With a view to sustaining student motivation and maximizing the effectiveness of our feedback, we combined teacher feedback with teacher–student conferencing and peer conferencing. Specifically, we paired a more proficient learner with a less proficient one and guided students in how to help each other reflect on their own writing by providing them with guidelines adopted from Hess (2001, p. 82).

Students received their guidelines, read peers' comments, and asked questions for clarification as needed. They then compared their classmate's comments with those of the teacher. To keep stronger learners from feeling that they did not benefit from this activity, we spent a few minutes with each one to help clarify, explain, or discuss their writing further.

Peer Writing

Our purpose in collaborative writing was for a more proficient peer to work with and assist a less proficient one. Peer writing encourages social interaction through which writers are guided gradually to solve problems that would normally be beyond their ability (H. D. Brown, 2001). In this class, peer writing was conducted through pair or group activities such as brainstorming, selecting and organizing ideas, and joint construction of texts under teacher supervision. To enhance the effectiveness of these activities, we carefully selected pairs or groups and assigned each member a specific role. For example, we asked more proficient learners to help their less proficient peers express their meanings in English by asking questions and modeling. We also took great care to establish a friendly learning environment in which students felt safe and willing to work together.

Peer Conferencing

Peer conferences were conducted to engage students in talking about their writing in order to learn from themselves and others (Campbell, 1999; Kroll, 2001). In conferencing, students were guided to share their work and help their peers reflect. They were not expected to correct errors, but to discuss how errors "impede their understanding of the texts" (Ferris, 2002, p. 329). Teachers can assist in this activity by providing learners with peer conference guidelines and monitoring their use. The guidelines should clearly state the purpose of the conference, the expectations for the parties involved, and the aspects of the essay they may want to consider discussing. The guidelines we used for our writing class are provided in Figures 3 and 4.

The purpose of this conference is to help you improve your writing and develop as a writer. Your classmate will help you reflect on your writing process, your problems, and your needs. Work with him or her by following these steps:

1. Tell your classmate what you think about your essay and what you want feedback on.

2. Read your essay to your classmate, or give it to him or her to read.

3. Ask your classmate for feedback, and make notes.

Consider these points before you start:

The things I like most about my essay are _____

The things I am not so sure about when writing this essay are _____

I need feedback on _____

Figure 3. Peer Conferencing Guidelines for the Writer

Your role in this conference is to help your classmate clarify or identify his or her writing problems. You can do so by sharing your feelings about the essay or asking your classmate questions about the essay. However, you do not need to correct it. Please be as supportive as possible!

Make some notes about your classmate's essay before you talk about it:

The things I like most about this essay are _____

I like them because _____

The things I would like to know more about are _____

The things I was confused about are _____

When reading your classmate's essay put a check mark in the appropriate box:

	Y	N
1. This essay has three main parts: introduction, body, and conclusion.	☐	☐
2. The introduction states the topic of the essay.	☐	☐
3. The body has more than one paragraph.	☐	☐
4. Each paragraph deals with one main idea only.	☐	☐
5. The conclusion summarizes the main ideas of the essay.	☐	☐
6. The ideas are relevant and supported by evidence and examples.	☐	☐
7. The ideas are developed from one paragraph to another.	☐	☐
8. The ideas are linked well together.	☐	☐
9. There are no spelling or grammar mistakes.	☐	☐

Figure 4. Peer Conferencing Guidelines for the Partner

REFLECTIONS

To have students evaluate their progress, an end-of-course questionnaire was designed (see the Appendix). The questionnaire, which was in the form of an attitude scale (Dörnyei, 2007; Karavas-Doukas, 1996; Seliger & Shohamy, 1989), comprised 15 statements focusing on students' self-assessment of their progress in composing a "reasoned text that is well-developed and supported with evidence and details" (Scarcella, 2002, p. 211) as well as their attitudes toward peer collaboration.

Data from the questionnaire indicate that students found the writing tasks more enjoyable and more effective when those tasks were scaffolded through collaboration between the teacher and students or among students. Such collaboration enabled all students to make progress; they were no longer left to sink or swim as in a traditional writing classroom. Scaffolding forms such as peer conferencing, collaborative writing, and the combination of teacher–student conferencing with written feedback motivated and engaged students of different levels and abilities.

It might be the case that for scaffolding to work effectively in a multilevel class, various types are needed depending on students' proficiency levels and stages of linguistic development. For example, modeling seemed to work better for more proficient students. Because they had acquired sufficient grammar and vocabulary, all they needed to know seemed to be how to organize their ideas and arguments effectively. Peer conferencing seemed to be more helpful for less proficient students. And teacher–student conferencing and written feedback apparently worked equally well for both types of students. Because different students had different problems and difficulties due to their different levels of proficiency, individual on-the-spot scaffolds provided by the teachers helped students move beyond their zone of proximal development and become independent writers more quickly.

According to Maybin, Mercer, and Stierer (1992), any particular example of help is considered to be scaffolding only if there is evidence of a learner successfully completing the task with the teacher's help and evidence of the learner having moved to a greater level of independent competence as a result of the experience. Students' perceptions of their progress in academic writing, their increased self-confidence, and their positive attitudes toward peer collaboration could serve well as these two kinds of evidence. Although there is no single solution to the issues presented by multilevel writing classes, and the evidence might have been more persuasively justified by analyzing students' performance on standardized tests, we believe scaffolding as a pedagogic strategy paid important dividends. Especially when resources are limited and students are of mixed abilities, scaffolding seems to be a solution that helps students "learn how to use one another as language resources" (Hess, 2001, p. 10). By incorporating scaffolding, teachers can avoid the inherent multilevel problem of stronger students feeling held back while weaker students feel pressured or lost. To be truly effective, scaffolding needs to be progressively adjusted to address the needs of different students within a single classroom.

Le Van Canh is a senior lecturer and teacher educator in applied linguistics in the College of Foreign Languages at Hanoi National University, in Vietnam. He has been a featured speaker at several international TESOL conferences, and his articles have appeared in Teacher's Edition, Asia TEFL Journal, *and elsewhere.*

Nguyen Thi Thuy Minh recently completed a PhD in applied linguistics at the University of Auckland. She is currently teaching in the College of Foreign Languages at Hanoi National University, in Vietnam. She is also a reviewing editor for Asian EFL Journal.

APPENDIX: STUDENT QUESTIONNAIRE

Part I. Self-Evaluation of Your Progress

Having completed this academic writing course, I:

1. know clearly how many parts an English essay is composed of.

1	2	3	4	5
strongly disagree		not sure		strongly agree

2. know how to write the introduction part of an essay appropriately.

1	2	3	4	5
strongly disagree		not sure		strongly agree

3. know how to write the multiparagraph development part of an essay appropriately.

1	2	3	4	5
strongly disagree		not sure		strongly agree

4. know how to write the conclusion part of an essay appropriately.

1	2	3	4	5
strongly disagree		not sure		strongly agree

5. know how to use discourse devices (linking words) in an essay better.

1	2	3	4	5
strongly disagree		not sure		strongly agree

6. know how to develop an outline for an essay (including generating and organizing ideas).

1	2	3	4	5
strongly disagree		not sure		strongly agree

7. know how to evaluate my own essay (including checking the organization of ideas, arguments, grammar, and vocabulary).

1	2	3	4	5
strongly disagree		not sure		strongly agree

8. feel confident that I can write an academic essay appropriately.

1	2	3	4	5
strongly disagree		not sure		strongly agree

9. feel that my writing skills have improved considerably.

1	2	3	4	5
strongly disagree		not sure		strongly agree

10. feel that I can write an academic essay much better than before.

1	2	3	4	5
strongly disagree		not sure		strongly agree

Part II. General Evaluation of the Course

11. The writing lessons had many pair or group activities (working together on generating ideas and giving feedback to peers).

1	2	3	4	5
strongly disagree		not sure		strongly agree

12. On the whole, I felt that the writing lessons were highly effective for me.

1	2	3	4	5
strongly disagree		not sure		strongly agree

13. I appreciated the support and assistance given by my teachers in the writing lessons.

1	2	3	4	5
strongly disagree		not sure		strongly agree

14. I found the writing tasks given by my teachers useful to me.

1	2	3	4	5
strongly disagree		not sure		strongly agree

15. I really enjoyed the writing lessons.

1	2	3	4	5
strongly disagree		not sure		strongly agree

CHAPTER 15

Self-Access
Language Learning:
Accommodating Diversity

Garold Murray

Self-access language learning has garnered attention because of its potential to respond to the range of levels and abilities that students bring to learning contexts. This chapter recounts how a classroom in northern Japan was transformed into a self-access center to accommodate the diverse needs of an urban community. The program put in place has been successful in offering learning opportunities to English language learners with multiple proficiency levels, mixed abilities, different learning styles, varying purposes, and a range of ages, but there has been an additional, unexpected outcome—the emergence of a community of practice. Wenger, McDermott, and Snyder (2002) tell us that

> a community of practice is a unique combination of three fundamental elements: a *domain* of knowledge, which defines a set of issues; a *community* of people who care about this domain; and the shared *practice* they are developing to be effective in their domain. (p. 27)

In this case, the self-access center has drawn together people from various walks of life who are passionate about deepening their knowledge and expertise in their use of English. These people come to the center regularly to engage in the learning practices offered in this environment. The presence of the constituent elements identified by Wenger et al., combined with prolonged engagement and social interaction on the part of the learners, has fostered the development of a community of practice.

What follows is a description of the learning structure that provides the framework for the practices of this community of learners. After setting the scene in northern Japan, I outline the features of the learning structure and then explain how this framework enables learners to create and carry out their own personal learning plans. I conclude by reflecting on the learners' experiences and considering the appropriateness of this learning structure for other contexts.

CONTEXT

The initiative to provide self-access language learning to the general public was inspired by Akita International University's (AIU) mission of service to the local community. AIU is a new, small university with a liberal arts curriculum delivered in English. Based on work that had been done at AIU to establish a self-access center and to implement a required course in self-directed language learning for all 1st-year students, the Japanese Ministry of Education awarded the university a 4-year grant to open a self-access center in the business district of the city of Akita. Although the center was to target the business community, it would be open to learners from all walks of life. Therefore, it had to meet the language learning needs of people with a wide range of purposes, language levels, abilities, and personal circumstances.

In response to this diversity, a learning structure has been put in place that combines principles of learner autonomy and elements of self-access language learning. I briefly outline here those that pertain to this project, but educators interested in a comprehensive overview of learner autonomy in language learning and self-access language learning should refer to Benson (2001, 2006) and Gardner and Miller (1999). My work in this case was also informed by Holec's (1981) model of learner autonomy, which calls for a learning structure to be put in place that enables learners to assume responsibility for all aspects of the learning process, including setting goals, choosing content, selecting methods, monitoring progress, and evaluating outcomes. In accordance with Holec's model, learners who come to the center each have their own personal learning plan. Furthermore, the learning structure aims to provide learners with opportunities to develop not only their language proficiency but also their metacognitive knowledge and skills. The learning structure also makes provision for learners to have support and guidance as they carry out their plans and access a learning environment with a wide range of resources.

The learning environment is shaped by several features. First and foremost, there are no teacher-directed language lessons. Learners improve their language proficiency by working directly with materials, most of which were originally intended for native English speakers. Among the materials are DVDs of movies and television programs, books with audio recordings, computer programs, reference materials, magazines, newspapers, music CDs, language proficiency test preparation materials, and other materials especially designed for foreign language learners.

Second, the learning is personalized. Learners set their own goals. They are encouraged to choose materials they find interesting and to work with them in ways that best suit them. Learners also plan and manage their learning. For example, they decide when they will come to the center, how long they will stay, and what they will do while they are there. These decisions, which in most school structures are made by administrators and teachers, are now the learners' responsibility. In fact, there are no "teachers" at the center. Teachers become language advisers whose prime role is to offer guidance and support to learners as they work on learning the language and developing their metacognitive skills.

Another important aspect of the learning environment is the physical layout and the atmosphere it creates. The space allocated for the project was a large classroom in a newly constructed multipurpose educational facility in the heart of the city. The intention underlying the physical design of the center was to create an inviting space that suggests a mode of learning different from the transmission model associated with the traditional classroom configuration. Therefore, the huge whiteboard that took up most of one wall was replaced with wooden display cabinets for materials. The opposite wall was lined with bookshelves (see Figure 1). Lounge-style armchairs formed a reading area, and others were grouped

Photo by Akihiro Miura.

Figure 1. Bookshelf Lining One Wall of the Center

around a widescreen television in one corner. Round café tables took the place of desks, and computers were placed on large round tables in the middle of the room (see Figure 2). The final touch was a glass door, which we hoped would provide a welcoming window onto a relaxed learning environment.

The learners who have been attracted to this environment range in age from 17 to 77. Approximately one-third of them are businesspeople or civil servants, and the other two-thirds are housewives and retired people. Their purposes vary from needing English for business or leisure travel to needing it to able to communicate with their grandchildren. High school students, who make up 10% of the learner population, want to pass university entrance examinations. The high school students—and, from time to time, other members—eventually move on, but as in any community, newcomers arrive to take their place.

Photo by Masataka Takahashi.

Figure 2. Learners in the Various Areas of the Center

CURRICULUM, TASKS, MATERIALS

Newcomers to the center are invited to attend an orientation session during which one of the bilingual staff members and I explain what the center offers and how it operates. We also give newcomers a bilingual booklet explaining what we mean by *independent language learning* (Murray & Cotterall, 2006). Following this explanation, we guide them through the process of developing their learning plans. However, before we begin, we ask each newcomer to complete a Learner Profile, which asks for information about his or her language learning history and encourages reflection on his or her language needs. The needs assessment part of the document consists of a list of things that can be done in English (e.g., listen to news programs, watch movies, read newspapers and magazines). Learners check off the things they would like to be able to do. When they finish, they choose three that they would like to start work on immediately.

Once the newcomer has completed a Learner Profile, he or she starts work on the learning plan. To facilitate this process, we provide a Personal Learning Plan form (see Appendix A). The first step is for learners to determine their goals. The needs assessment section of the Learner Profile has laid the groundwork for this important decision; if learners wish, they can choose their goals from among the three items they identified as their priorities.

Once learners have set their goals, they need to choose materials. After pointing out different materials available in the center, we work with each person to suggest several options that would be appropriate for his or her goals. For example, if a beginning-level learner chooses as a goal "to improve listening to daily conversations," we would suggest one of the interactive computer programs that focus on everyday communication situations. Intermediate- or advanced-level learners might be shown DVDs and novels accompanied by audio recordings.

After learners have chosen materials that match their goals, they decide how they are going to use them to learn English. At the center, we have developed a series of strategy guides in English and bilingual formats that offer suggestions for using the materials. For example, DVDs of movies and television programs are popular choices, so we have developed a strategy guide that suggests ways for learners to use DVDs for effective development of listening skills (see Appendix B). Learners are encouraged to experiment with different strategies, adapt the strategies to suit their learning styles, and eventually devise their own strategies.

The assessment section of the Personal Learning Plan is completed when learners finish working with the materials or decide to revise their plan. This section provides them with an opportunity to reflect: What did they learn? How do they know? What would they do differently next time? Did they learn anything about how to learn a language? Once learners have completed this section, they create a new learning plan.

In addition to assessing their learning at the end of an activity, learners are encouraged to monitor it on a daily basis. We explain that to monitor means to keep learning under observation, to be focused on what they are doing and how they are doing it, to look critically at the learning, and to be ready to make changes to their learning plans when necessary. To support learners, we provide them with a Daily Learning Log form (see Appendix C), on which they document what they do during each visit, their reflection on the experience, and what they plan to do during their next visit. The Personal Learning Plan helps learners structure their learning over the long term, and the Daily Learning Log helps them monitor their learning on a regular, more immediate basis.

The Daily Learning Log, Personal Learning Plan, and Learner Profile, along with other items that may provide evidence of learning, are kept in a portfolio. A review of the portfolio can help learners assess progress and provide insights into how their thinking about language learning is developing (Yang, 2003). In addition, the records contained in the portfolio are quite useful when learners request advising sessions.

Advising sessions are a crucial form of support. They are mostly instigated by learners who may be having some difficulty, want to talk about their learning, or would like guidance as they revise their learning plans. (For more information on language advising, see Kelly, 1996; Mozzon-McPherson, 2000). In addition to advising sessions, the center offers a series of workshops on a variety of topics, including learning strategies, reading, writing, and monitoring and assessment strategies.

Another form of support and guidance comes from the learners themselves. They have reported in interviews conducted as a part of a long-term study exploring their experiences in the center that being surrounded by other people with similar interests and goals is a source of support and motivation. Although they work independently, they do not work in isolation. Regularly scheduled activities such as conversation group meetings not only provide learners with opportunities to practice their oral skills but enable them to socialize and talk about their learning. It is not unusual for such conversations to be continued over coffee elsewhere. The social aspects of the center are reinforced by events such as Christmas parties and cherry blossom viewing picnics, which are organized by staff in collaboration with learners.

REFLECTIONS

The self-access center has been successful in providing language learning opportunities to a diverse group of people. This conclusion is supported by monthly statistics compiled on learners' use of the center and the findings of an ethnographic research project we have been conducting for the past 2 years. However, measuring the success of the center in terms of gains in language proficiency is problematic—there are no standardized tests. Furthermore, there are too many intervening variables. For the most part, learners are highly autonomous and engage in a variety of language learning activities in addition to their work in the center. Even so, our study indicates that they find their own ways of measuring their progress. For example, one learner reports being able to speak more fluently in discussion groups, and another notes increased comprehension in the workshops. Rather than measure progress by test scores, the center offers certificates for the number of hours of independent language learning completed. Whether the certificates are presented for the initial 30 hours of learning or, most recently, for 400, 500, and 600 hours of learning, the recipients are celebrated by the other learners.

Perhaps the center's greatest success is the community of learners that has evolved. And though they benefit from the support that comes from being part of a community of people with similar goals engaged in shared practices, the learners also appreciate the autonomy that the learning structure affords them. One housewife said, "I can study English with my own will, at my pace, without thinking about some other people's pace or speed." A civil servant said he appreciated the flexibility that enabled him to fit English language learning into his hectic work schedule. The learning structure makes it possible for learners to work at their own pace, with materials appropriate for their language level, in ways that suit them, and at times they determine. The success of the center can be attributed to this learning structure that enables learners to personalize their learning, that is, to adapt it to suit their personal identities and the circumstances these identities engender.

There is evidence to suggest that this learning structure can be adapted to meet the needs of multilevel, mixed-ability groups of language learners in institutional settings ranging from elementary to tertiary levels of education. At AIU this learning structure forms the basis of a course in self-directed language learning for students in the English for Academic Purposes Program. Furthermore, there are reports of cases in which self-access learning has been successfully integrated into the curriculum at the high school level in Thailand (Darasawong, Singhasiri, & Keyuravong, 2007), Japan (Hale, 2006), and Malaysia (L. Miller, 1999). In Denmark, classroom-based instruction promoting learner autonomy has given middle school children opportunities to structure, manage, and assess their language learning (Dam, 1995). Similarly, research carried out in the United States exploring a community-of-learners model supports the contention that, given proper support, even young learners can take responsibility for their learning in classrooms that foster autonomy (Rogoff, 1994).

Regardless of the setting in which this type of learning structure is introduced, one possible issue could be the willingness of educators to permit learners to take control of their learning. Commenting on the implementation of the community-of-learning model that also fosters learner autonomy, Rogoff (1994) describes the change required in the mind-set of educators as "a paradigm shift like that of learning how to function in another culture" (p. 215). Not only do teachers have to take on new roles, but they have to trust and honor learners' understandings of how they learn. Rather than impose their understanding of how learning takes place, teachers need to accept learners' beliefs about how they learn as a starting point for the work. As a facilitator, the teacher's role is to provide learners with opportunities to expand their metacognitive awareness and knowledge. Over time, witnessing learners' linguistic and metacognitive development should assuage teachers' fears about learners taking charge of their own learning.

What does the learning structure outlined in this chapter tell teachers about meeting the needs of learners in multilevel, mixed-ability settings? In the first place, it tells them that learners can benefit from a learning environment that fosters their autonomy. Second, learners should be able to personalize their learning, that is, set goals that are meaningful to them, select materials that they find interesting, and work with the materials in ways that suit their identities. Third, learners can take responsibility for their learning when they have appropriate support and guidance. And finally, learners can and will support one another. In this case, a learning structure informed by principles of learner autonomy and elements of self-access learning enabled learners to adapt the learning to their individual needs and fostered the emergence of a community of learners.

Garold Murray is currently developing self-access and e-learning programs at Okayama University, in Japan. Prior to this, he worked at Akita International University, where he established the center discussed in this chapter. His research employs narrative inquiry to explore learner autonomy in language learning in classroom, out-of-class, and self-access contexts.

APPENDIX A: PERSONAL LEARNING PLAN

Name　氏名: _____

Date started　開始日: _____ / _____ / _____

Date finished/stopped　終了日: _____ / _____ / _____

できるだけ英語で記入して下さい

Goal(s) 目標:
Materials 教材:
Activity/Strategies: How will you use this material to help you meet your goals? Please be specific. For example, list the activities in order: 1st, 2nd, 3rd, etc. 学習/ストラテジー：あなたの目標を達成するために、この教材をどのようにつかっていくかを具体的に記入してください。箇条書で記入してください
Assessment: When you finish this material or decide to change your goals, material, or strategies, please write about your experience. For example, how enjoyable did you find the activity you completed? Do you feel you learned something? How do you know? What would you do differently next time? 評価：あなたの使っていた教材が終了し、あなたのゴール、教材、ストラテジーを変えるときは、ここにあなたの学習履歴を記入してください。例：どれくらい楽しんで学習することができたか、次回は何を学習したいのか、など

APPENDIX B: STRATEGY GUIDE FOR WATCHING (LISTENING TO) DVDS

To learn English from DVDs of movies or television programs, it is necessary to listen to the same movie or television program more than one time. Below are suggestions for listening at three different levels of difficulty. You choose the level that best matches your ability to understand. You also can combine these suggestions in different ways to create a method that works best for you.

Advanced Level

1. Listen to the English soundtrack with English subtitles.

2. Listen to the English soundtrack with Japanese subtitles. [Only do this to check your comprehension.]

3. Listen to the English soundtrack only. [No subtitles.]

Intermediate Level

1. Listen to the English with Japanese subtitles.

2. Listen to the English with English subtitles.

3. Listen to the English only. [No subtitles.]

Basic Level

1. Listen to the Japanese soundtrack.

2. Listen to the English with Japanese subtitles.

3. Listen to English with English subtitles.

During the first and second listenings, it is best not to listen all the way through. Rather, break it up into scenes or segments. For example, listen to a scene (2–3 minutes) in English with Japanese subtitles, then listen to the same scene in English with English subtitles, and then either proceed to the next scene or listen to the same scene for a third time with the English soundtrack only. When you finish, you could watch the whole movie again in English with no subtitles, or you might choose to listen to the movie in English with English subtitles.

If you choose to use the method suggested for the Basic Level, it is best if you start out using a short television program. Movies are too long as a language learning activity—they take too much time for you to work through properly. As your listening skills improve, you can start working with movies.

APPENDIX C: DAILY LEARNING LOG

Name 氏名: _____   ※できるだけ英語で記入してください

Date 日付
How long you did spend on task? 今日はどのくらい学習しましたか？
Materials: What did you do with the materials? Please be specific. 使った教材: どのように教材を使いましたか？具体的に記入してください
Reflection: What did you learn? What difficulties did you have? Other comments/thoughts? 感想：反省を記入してください
Question: Do you have any questions about your learning that you would like to discuss? 質問：今日学んだことで質問があれば記入してください
Planning: What will you do next time? 計画：次回の学習計画を立てましょう

CHAPTER 16

Building a Community of Mixed-Ability Learners: Connect, Network, Empower

Jo Bertrand

I recently taught business communication English to a class of Chinese nuclear engineers and communicative teaching methods to Chinese secondary school English teachers. Despite the markedly different teaching contexts, I found that both groups of learners posed similar problems: They both had a wide range of linguistic abilities and professional statuses. To overcome these challenges, I developed a "connect, network, and empower" approach to setting up the classroom and classroom tasks. I wanted to ensure that the learning experience was positive for all learners and not influenced by their professional contexts outside the classroom. In this chapter, I explore ways of building a community of mixed-level, mixed-status learners who can work effectively together.

CONTEXT

Teacher Training Course

The first teaching context was a teacher training course that was set up by the British Council and local education authorities in northern China. I was one of three British Council consultants, and together we trained a total of 90 English language school teachers full time for 4 weeks. The participants mostly lived in small villages dotted around the city of Dalian, teaching English with limited resources to classes of up to 80 students. Some of them already knew each other and taught in the same school. In the first class, a female teacher spoke up to welcome one of her colleagues; the woman she introduced had actually been her own teacher at school.

With this declaration came respect but also tension. The younger teacher and her peers needed to do their best in front of the more senior teachers, and the more senior teachers, who struggled linguistically, needed to prove their language ability in front of their younger colleagues. The better English speakers were not necessarily the more experienced professionally. This could have led to reluctance to show up the weaker yet more experienced teachers and embarrassment from those less able to express themselves.

Business Communication Course

The business communication course lasted for a total of 24 hours over the course of 3 months. The class took place two evenings a week at the nuclear power plant near the southern Chinese city of Shenzhen. The variations in students' language ability were immense. They ranged from a complete beginner, who was unable to give his name in English, to the Human Resources Department interpreter. Another challenge was the mix of workers and managers of all levels. In some cultures, this scenario may not be an issue because senior managers often have private tutoring and thus do not join mixed classes. In smaller companies, the corporate culture may be such that hierarchy is less defined. In my experience in China, however, I found that this mix created potential occasions for embarrassment and losing face, which could have ultimately resulted in learners being reluctant to communicate for fear of humiliating themselves or others. W. Hu and Grove (1991) confirm this notion when they refer to Chinese learners' "reluctance to speak" (p. 69), and Ouyang's (2004) research shows that Chinese students tend not to ask questions in class in order to avoid either themselves or the teacher losing face.

With these learners, I wanted to take the focus away from me as the teacher so as to enable them to have as much speaking time as possible. Gao and Liu (2005) highlight the need for this by describing "the silent behaviour of Chinese students," "the norm of being a good listener in order to be a good student," and how "the teacher does almost all of the speaking in class" (pp. 108–111). Because this was a communication course, it was imperative that the learners felt comfortable enough to speak. But this would be a challenge because, for example, in the first class some of the recently graduated engineers discreetly expressed their concern about talking in English in front of their manager.

CURRICULUM, TASKS, MATERIALS

It was essential to establish a safe environment (Hess, 2001) whereby the classes could gel and have meaningful exchanges. I had to devise an approach that took learners' linguistic and professional differences into consideration and gave them adequate space to learn without them developing a sense of abandonment. I wanted to guide them without dominating them. I wanted to bring the best out of them and give them confidence to work together. I used three principles to bring together these communities of mixed-ability and mixed-status learners: connect, network, and empower.

Connect

In both teaching scenarios, I had neither the time nor the resources to carry out a precourse level test or needs analysis to determine groups. Nevertheless, I wanted to find out about the learners as quickly as possible and help them connect with each other. I therefore allocated time in the first business communication lesson for learners to fill out a simple questionnaire that I had adapted from *Teaching Business English* (M. Ellis & Johnson, 1994). This questionnaire referred directly to the contact learners had with English speakers and what exactly they wanted to work on. I included questions such as these:

- Whom do you talk to in English?

- Where do you talk to them most—in a group meeting, on the phone, face to face?

- Why can it be difficult to communicate with them?

The only information I had received was that course participants wanted to work on their speaking. I needed to create a bonded community and give students a reason to care about their colleagues. They did not all work in the same department, so for some there was a sense of unfamiliarity and a fear of the unknown. The context of an English classroom alone was new to some of them. For those who did work in the same office, the issue of professional ranking had to be addressed. The questionnaire results served to demonstrate common objectives, which was essential for connecting the group and giving them a sense of belonging. In the second lesson, I communicated their main objectives back to them, demonstrating that despite their backgrounds and levels they were all traveling in the same direction—toward more effective oral communication. They wanted to overcome their apprehension about talking to their foreign associates and be able to express themselves more precisely.

Also in the teacher training course, the teachers completed a questionnaire in the first session. I adapted a "Getting to Know You" worksheet from *Teachers in Action* (James, 2001) so that all the teachers could respond with as little or as much language as they wanted. The questions were fairly straightforward, asking, for example, what they did and did not enjoy about being a teacher and why they had become teachers. We all mingled and found someone with similar likes and dislikes, and thus were quickly able to connect with each other.

Network

Where students sit, when they sit, how long they sit, and whom they sit with are key factors when creating a caring community. I changed where they sat as much as possible. They started each lesson at a new table, and very quickly they were made to work with as many people as possible. If students always sit with the same people, their community may consist of only themselves and one other person. It is not a case of wanting to stop them from connecting with another person, but of allowing them to network with the entire class.

In addition, I never sat down. I made it my business to be mobile and discreetly physically present everywhere—creating invisible, reassuring boundaries for the community. Figure 1 shows how I rearranged the class of engineers using the tables to create minicommunities. Although I was aware as the course progressed that friendships were forming, I encouraged interaction with all class members regardless of age, level, or status. I needed these differences to be eradicated for the newly formed community of mixed learners to work together successfully.

Notice that the tables are all pointing toward the whiteboard, which meant that no one had their back to the front. This way, students all had equal access to the board without being put in the hot seat, and neither could they hide away in a corner. It was also important to make the learning environment as far removed as possible from the individual seats in rows that these Chinese learners may have associated with school.

By changing the physical environment I let learners know that I, the teacher, was not the focus. By being arranged in smaller groups, students could see that they would have to communicate with others rather than look at the back of someone's head. By changing where they sat each lesson, I helped students quickly become familiar with all class members; thus they all felt part of a community. And by changing partners regularly, students engaged in richer exchanges among different levels.

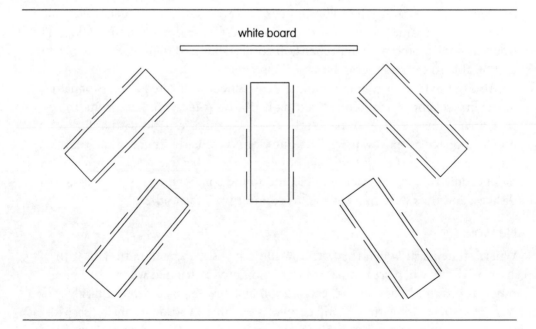

Figure 1. Table Arrangement to Facilitate Forming Small Learning Communities

Empower

Empower in this case means enabling learners to take control of their learning, take the lead in a group situation, and become more confident language learners. In a language classroom with students of mixed proficiency levels and statuses, it is especially important to establish equality early on, because without equality they cannot be empowered. For students to be equal, it is important that everyone has the same level of understanding, so I began the business communication course with a simple bonding activity that everyone could follow: Everyone stood in a circle, straightaway forming a physical, visual community. I was also part of that circle as a community member, not as the leader. Each person said his or her name and did an action at the same time. Once we had been round the circle twice, the challenge was to repeat somebody else's name and action. The workers and managers were equal in terms of their understanding and actions because they were not solely relying on linguistic skills. By incorporating paralanguage and other skills such as memory into activities, all learners had equal opportunities to express themselves. In his article about multilevel classes, J. Rose (1997) says that "both linguistic and non-linguistic skills" should be valued so that "everyone can contribute" (p. 4).

With the learners in the teacher training course, the process of empowerment presented different complications. Some were visibly at ease in a leading position, but this was not the case for all of them and I needed the less assertive among them to feel as in control as their peers. For this course, I wrote a short song about teaching teenagers and used it as the warm-up activity. I wanted all the learners to be active at once, and I needed to set the tone of the course. As they stood up and sang an action song, they were using their bodies to express themselves and not merely relying on their linguistic abilities or professional backgrounds to be able to achieve the task. With this song, I gave visual, auditory, and kinesthetic learners equal opportunities to understand and participate. I continued to empower learners throughout both courses in the following ways:

- clearly demonstrating every activity and checking understanding through volunteer learner demonstration

- discreetly monitoring for lack of understanding where most needed so that lower level learners did not feel abandoned

- having learners change partners so that less proficient students could also lead and not always be led and so that stronger students could help their peers as well as be challenged themselves

- giving everyone an opportunity to use newly learned language

- involving them in the course content and really listening to and incorporating their needs whenever possible

Business Communication Course

For this course, I chose to work with an intermediate-level textbook that is aimed at business English students and professionals who need English to communicate on a daily basis. I was confident that with the correct adaptation, *Working in English* (Jones, 2001) would be appropriate for a mixed-ability class. It concentrates on authentic, personalized oral communication for pair or group situations and provides frequent key phrases that can be integrated and reviewed throughout the course. Lower level students are supported through the buildup to freer communication, and higher level students are challenged through the use of authentic listening texts. The task described here is a telephone role-play that I chose because on the needs analysis questionnaire many of the participants had cited telephone calls as one of the most difficult aspects of communication with their foreign counterparts.

For the warm-up, we began the lesson as a whole group to help the learners connect. On the telephone, they all had to understand numbers, dates, and prices, so on the whiteboard I wrote the numbers 1 through 10. I asked the learners to copy them, and I then turned the whiteboard around so that only I could see it. I exaggerated a demonstration of how they should keep their papers secret from others. Rather than individualizing the activity, this unites class members and makes them laugh together. I then went through numbers 1–3, for each saying a price, date, or telephone number, and I simultaneously wrote down what I said. They had to listen and write down what they heard. To make sure everyone had an equal chance of getting the correct answer, I repeated each one at least twice. (This was merely practice for the role-play that was to follow, because during that activity they would need to listen for details.) Then they looked to see if their classmates had the same answer. I then turned the whiteboard around so that everyone could check their answers. I turned the board back around and asked for a volunteer to call out the remaining numbers, prices, and dates. Once they had done this as a class, I assigned a "teacher" at each table to lead the activity in his or her group. This warm-up encompassed all three principles of my framework: The learners connected with each other through fun, networked through the sharing of answers, and were empowered by adopting the role of teacher.

For the role-play itself, the activity and checklist (see Figure 2) were taken from *Working in English* (Jones, 2001, p. 23). This telephone dialogue has three roles: two speaking and one observing. The implication is that learners are empowered because they all have the opportunity to observe and give feedback to their peers about the effectiveness of their role-play conversation. For learners to observe and give feedback appropriately, they had a checklist of dos and don'ts. Before embarking on the activity itself, they practiced using the checklist by listening to a couple of prerecorded telephone dialogues.

I chose this particular role-play because it required learners to listen for details such as shipment dates and quantities of products, which was relevant to the learners' actual work environment.

While making a phone call . . .	Dialogue 1	Dialogue 2	Dialogue 3
Tell the other person who you are and why you're calling			
Speak clearly and not too fast			
Speak in a polite and friendly tone of voice			
Make notes on the important information			
Ask the person to repeat anything you aren't sure about			
Double-check your notes to make sure they're correct			
Finish the call in a positive, friendly way			

Source: Jones, 2001, p. 23.

Figure 2. Telephone Dialogue Role-Play Checklist

As mentioned earlier, seating is vital. For a telephone conversation, I have the two speakers sit back to back, with their chairs touching, and the observer sit in the middle but facing both speakers. The few minutes it takes to rearrange the chairs is worth it to allow a more realistic situation in which there are no visual clues to aid understanding, just as when you actually speak on the phone.

Teacher Training Course

I divided learners in the teacher training course into different sessions, including Large Classes, Drama Workshop, and Getting Your Teenagers to Talk. I always used activities that the teachers could take away and try out with their own students. Here I describe a discussion activity that I used in the Large Classes session.

The teachers first came up with a list of subjects that their teenage students would be interested in. Together, we brainstormed useful vocabulary about each of the subjects. I then split the class into two groups. They stood in two concentric circles—the inner circle facing out, the outer circle facing in. I told them the first subject and gave them 1 minute to talk to the person in front of them. After one minute, I called, "Change." The outer circle moved one space to the right. The inner circle remained where they were. An alternative would be to provide simple but provocative statements such as "School uniforms should be compulsory" or "Art is an easy subject." One can also preteach expressions for students to use, such as "What do you think about . . . ?" and "As far as I'm concerned . . . ." In any case, the subjects should be relevant to learners so that when they communicate they can connect. In this activity, learners talk to many classmates, so they are networking and mixing with all levels and backgrounds.

Learners should all have an equal understanding of the needed language. It does not matter if the language they produce is not as good as that of their partners—the objective is for everyone to have opportunities to speak and use the language they have learned. In this case, I empowered learners through demonstration so that they all had a clear understanding of what they had to do.

REFLECTIONS

By using a "connect, network, and empower" approach to teaching, I was able to build two communities of learners. In both teaching contexts, the upper-intermediate learners willingly helped their elementary peers. The lower level students overcame their inhibitions, and the higher level students adopted a leadership role—regardless of their professional status. Through natural, human collaboration they helped and challenged one another to achieve their linguistic goals. At the end of the teacher training course, one of the school teachers presented me with a notebook in which she had written a long, touching message that, thanks to the course, she would be able to take risks in her future teaching. She explained how the course had been a "safe and comfortable environment" and how she had been able to rebuild her confidence as both a teacher and a language learner.

In the Chinese classroom, learners naturally cooperate with each other. Nelson (1995) suggests that under the influence of Confucian tradition, Chinese learners support each other as they strive for "group harmony" (p. 9). Teaching these mixed-ability and mixed-status classes could have been a struggle, but by building on their willingness to collaborate and establishing an unthreatening community, all learners had equal opportunities to learn, progress, experiment, and achieve. Their professional statuses outside the classroom became insignificant inside the classroom, and their language levels were relevant only as a measure of the progress that they made.

Jo Bertrand has been involved in English language teaching for 14 years as a teacher, teacher trainer, examiner, and materials writer in England, China, Indonesia, and France. She has been working with the British Council since 2001, and she gives regular teacher development seminars for Cambridge ESOL.

References

Abrahams, R. D., & Troike, R. C. (Eds.). (1972). *Language and cultural diversity in American education.* Englewood Cliffs, NJ: Prentice Hall.

Adamson, A., & Jenson, V. (Directors). (2001). *Shrek* [Motion picture]. United States: DreamWorks.

Al-Jarf, R. (2006). Large student enrollments in EFL programs: Challenges and consequences. *Asian EFL Journal, 8*(4). Retrieved May 17, 2009, from http://www.asian-efl-journal.com/Dec_06_raj.php

Allwright, D. (1989). *Is class size a problem? Lancaster-Leeds Language Learning in Large Classes Research Project* (Project Report No. 3). Leeds, England: Lancaster-Leeds Language Learning in Large Classes Research Project. (ERIC Document Reproduction Service No. ED322754)

Allwright, D. (2005). From teaching points to learning opportunities and beyond. *TESOL Quarterly, 39,* 9–31.

Ariza, E. N. W. (2006). *Not for ESOL Teachers: What every classroom teacher needs to know about the linguistically, culturally, and ethnically diverse student.* New York: Pearson.

Atkinson, D. (1997). A critical approach to critical thinking in TESOL. *TESOL Quarterly, 31,* 71–94.

Audacity (Version 1.3) [Computer software]. (2009). Sourceforge. http://audacity.sourceforge.net

Bachman, L. (1990). *Fundamental considerations in language testing.* New York: Oxford University Press.

Baker, J., & Westrup, H. (2000). *The English language teacher's handbook: How to teach large classes with few resources.* London: Continuum.

Baker, J., & Westrup, H. (2003). *Essential speaking skills.* London: Continuum.

Barrera, I., & Kramer, L. (1997). From monologues to skilled dialogues: Teaching the process of crafting culturally competent early childhood environments. In P. J. Winton, J. A. McCollum, & C. Catlett (Eds.), *Reforming personnel preparation in early intervention: Issues, models, and practical strategies* (pp. 217–251). Baltimore: Paul H. Brookes.

Bassano, S., & Christison, M. A. (1995). *Community spirit: A practical guide to collaborative language learning*. San Francisco: Alta Book Center.

Baurain, B. (2005, November/December). Solving the multilevel dilemma. *ESL Magazine, 48,* 12–15.

Baurain, B. (2007). Small group multitasking in literature classes. *ELT Journal, 61,* 237–245.

Bell, J. (1991). *Teaching multilevel classes in ESL*. San Diego, CA: Dominie Press.

Bell, J. (1994). The challenges of multilevel classes. *Mosaic, 2*(1), 1, 3–5.

Bell, J. S. (2004). *Teaching multilevel classes in ESL* (2nd ed.). Toronto, Ontario, Canada: Pippin.

Benson, P. (2001). *Teaching and researching autonomy in language learning*. London: Longman.

Benson, P. (2006). Autonomy in language teaching and learning. *Language Teaching, 40,* 21–40.

Betella, A. (2007). Podcast generator (Version 1.2) [Computer software]. http://podcastgen.sourceforge.net

Bonwell, C. C., & Eison, J. A. (1991). *Active learning: Creating excitement in the classroom* (ASHE-ERIC Higher Education Report No. 1). Washington, DC: George Washington University, School of Education and Human Development.

Brown, H. D. (2001). *Teaching by principles: An interactive approach to language pedagogy* (2nd ed.). New York: Longman.

Brown, H. D. (2007). *Teaching by principles: An interactive approach to language pedagogy* (3rd ed.). Englewood Cliffs, NJ: Prentice Hall Regents.

Bruner, J. C. (1980). *The social context of language acquisition*. Princeton, NJ: Educational Testing Service.

Campbell, C. (1999). *Teaching second language writing: Interacting with text*. Boston: Heinle & Heinle.

Canagarajah, A. S. (1999). *Resisting linguistic imperialism in English teaching*. Oxford: Oxford University Press.

Canagarajah, A. S. (2002). *A geopolitics of academic writing*. New Delhi, India: Orient Longman.

Canagarajah, A. S. (2005). *Reclaiming the local in language policy and practice.* Mahwah, NJ: Lawrence Erlbaum.

Cary, S. (2004). *Going graphic: Comics at work in the multilingual classroom.* Portsmouth, NH: Heinemann.

Casanave, C. P. (2002). *Writing games: Multicultural case studies of academic literacy practices in higher education.* London: Lawrence Erlbaum.

Cazden, C. B. (2001). *Classroom discourse: The language of teaching and learning* (2nd ed.). Portsmouth, NH: Heinemann.

Coffin, C., Curry, M. J., Goodman, S., Hewings, A., Lillis, T. M., & Swann, S. (2003). *Teaching academic writing: A toolkit for higher education.* London: Routledge.

Coleman, H. (1989). *The study of large classes. Lancaster-Leeds Language Learning in Large Classes Research Project* (Project Report No. 2). Leeds, England: Lancaster-Leeds Language Learning in Large Classes Research Project. (ERIC Document Reproduction Service No. ED424045)

Coles, R. (1997). *Doing documentary work.* New York: Oxford University Press.

Collier, J., Jr., & Collier, M. (1986). *Visual anthropology: Photography as a research method.* Albuquerque: University of New Mexico Press.

Cotterall, S., & Cohen, R. (2003). Scaffolding for second language writers. *ELT Journal, 57,* 158–166.

Cross, W. E., Jr., Strauss, L., & Fhagen-Smith, P. (1999). African American identity development across the life span: Education implications. In R. Sheets & E. Hollins (Eds.), *Racial and ethnic identity in school practice: Aspects of human development* (pp. 29–47). Mahwah, NJ: Lawrence Erlbaum.

Cruz, P. (2007). *U.S. top selling computer hardware for January 2007.* Retrieved May 18, 2009, from http://www.bloomberg.com/apps/news?pid=conewsstory&refer=co news&tkr=AAPL:US&sid=ap0bqJw2VpwI

Curtain, H. A., & Dahlberg, C. A. (2004). *Languages and children: Making the match* (3rd ed.). Boston: Pearson.

Dam, L. (1995). *Learner autonomy 3: From theory to classroom practice.* Dublin, Ireland: Authentik.

Darasawong, P., Singhasiri, W., & Keyuravong, S. (2007). Developing student support in self-access centres. In A. Barfield & S. Brown (Eds.), *Reconstructing autonomy in language education: Inquiry and innovation* (pp. 167–179). Basingstoke, England: Palgrave Macmillan.

Davis, R. (1997). TV commercial messages: An untapped video resource for content-based classes. *Language Teacher, 21*(3), 13–15.

Day, R. (2003). Teaching critical thinking and discussion. *Language Teacher, 27*(7), 25–27.

DelliCarpini, M. (2006). Scaffolding and differentiating instruction in mixed ability ESL classes using a round robin activity. *Internet TESL Journal, 12*(3). Retrieved May 21, 2009, from http://iteslj.org/Techniques/DelliCarpini-RoundRobin.html

Devadason, I. (1997). *"Doing" reading in English.* Bangalore, India: National Printing Press.

Din, F. S. (1998). *The functions of class size perceived by Chinese rural school teachers.* Buffalo, NY: Research Forum of the National Rural Education Association. Retrieved April 3, 2009, from http://www.eric.ed.gov/ERICDocs/data/ericdocs2sql/content_storage_01/0000019b/80/16/f3/63.pdf

Dörnyei, Z. (2001). *Motivational strategies in the language classroom.* Cambridge: Cambridge University Press.

Dörnyei, Z. (2007). *Research methods in applied linguistics.* Oxford: Oxford University Press.

Echevarria, J., Vogt, M. E., & Short, D. J. (2004). *Making content comprehensible for English learners: The SIOP model* (2nd ed.). Boston: Pearson.

Edouard, G. (2006). Helping students improve their speaking skills through group work in EFL large classes. Unpublished project, School for International Training, Brattleboro, VT.

Edwards, V. (1999). Teaching and learning styles in multi-ethnic classrooms. In A. Tosi & C. Leung (Eds.), *Rethinking language education: From a monolingual to a multilingual perspective* (pp. 213–224). London: CILT.

Ellis, M., & Johnson, C. (1994). *Teaching business English.* Oxford: Oxford University Press.

Ellis, R. (1986). *Understanding second language acquisition.* Oxford: Oxford University Press.

Erkaya, O. R. (2005). TV commercials as authentic tools to teach communication, culture and critical thinking. *MexTESOL Journal, 29,* 13–25.

Ewald, W., & Lightfoot, A. (2001). *I'm gonna take me a picture: Teaching photography and writing to children.* Boston: Beacon Press.

Fassler, R. (1998). Peer support for getting into English in an ESL kindergarten. *Early Childhood Research Quarterly, 13,* 379–409.

Ferris, D. (2002). Teaching students to self-edit. In J. C. Richards & W. A. Renandya (Eds.), *Methodology in language teaching: An anthology of current practice* (pp. 328–334). Cambridge: Cambridge University Press.

Ferris, D. (2004). The "grammar correction" debate in L2 writing: Where are we, and where do we go from here? (And what do we do in the meantime . . . ?). *Journal of Second Language Writing, 13*, 49–62.

Fower, L. (1994). *The construction of negotiated meaning: A social cognitive theory of writing.* Carbondale: Southern Illinois University Press.

Gahin, G. M. A., & Mylill, D. A. (2003). The communicative approach in Egypt: Digging into the pyramids. In J. Gollin, G. Ferguson, & H. Trappes-Lomax (Eds.), *Symposium for language teacher educators.* Edinburgh: University of Edinburgh, IALS.

Gao, L., & Liu, J. (2005). When group work doesn't work: How can I engage students who don't participate? *Review of Applied Linguistics in China, 1*, 106–117.

GarageBand (Version 5.0.1) [Computer software]. (2009). Cupertino, CA: Apple. http://www.apple.com/ilife/garageband

Gardner, D., & Miller, L. (1999). *Establishing self-access: From theory to practice.* Cambridge: Cambridge University Press.

Gay, G. (2000). *Culturally responsive teaching: Theory, research, and practice.* New York: Teachers College Press.

Gibbons, P. (2002). *Scaffolding language, scaffolding learning: Teaching second language learners in the mainstream classroom.* Portsmouth, NH: Heinemann.

Gibbons, P. (2003). Mediating language learning: Teacher interactions with ESL students in a content-based classroom. *TESOL Quarterly, 37*, 247–273.

Goldthorpe, J. (1993, March). *Talking back to TV: Media literacy and writing.* Paper presented at the annual meeting of the Conference on College Composition and Communication, San Diego, CA. (ERIC Document Reproduction Service No. ED363880)

Gonzalez, N., Moll, L., & Amanti, C. (Eds.). (2005). *Funds of knowledge.* Mahwah, NJ: Lawrence Erlbaum.

Google. (2009). *Google video.* Retrieved May 18, 2009, from http://video.google.com/

Grant, C. A., & Sleeter, C. E. (2007). *Doing multicultural education for achievement and equity.* New York: Routledge.

Hale, C. (2006). Challenging tradition: Establishing a self-access language learning centre in an East Asian academic high school (Japan). In T. S. C. Farrell (Ed.), *Language teacher research in Asia* (pp. 75–90). Alexandria, VA: TESOL.

Hall, E. T. (1959). *The silent language.* Garden City, NY: Anchor Books.

Hamann, E. T., & Reeves, J. (2008, April). *Accessing high-quality instructional strategies.* Davis: University of California-Davis, School of Education, Center for Applied Policy in Education. Retrieved September 12, 2009, from http://cap-ed .ucdavis.edu/sites/cap-ed.ucdavis.edu/files/Hamann Paper WEB .pdf

Hannafin, M., Land, S., & Oliver, K. (1999). Open learning environment: Foundations, methods, and models. In C. Reigeluth (Ed.), *Instructional design theories and models* (Vol. 2, pp. 115–140). Mahwah, NJ: Lawrence Erlbaum.

Hardwick, H. C. (1968). *Words are important.* Allahabad, India: Wheeler.

Harrington, D., & LeBeau, C. (1996). *Speaking of speech: Basic presentation skills for beginners.* Tokyo: Macmillan Language House.

Harmin, M., & Toth, M. (2006). *Inspiring active learning: A complete handbook for today's teachers* (2nd ed.). Alexandria, VA: Association for Supervision and Curriculum Development.

Hayashi, C. (2005). *Scaffolding the academic writing process: A focus on developing ideas.* Retrieved May 21, 2009, from http://jalt.org/pansig/2005/HTML/ Hayashi.htm

He, A. E. (2005). Learning and teaching English in the People's Republic of China. In G. Braine (Ed.), *Teaching English to the world: History, curriculum, and practice* (pp. 11–22). Mahwah, NJ: Lawrence Erlbaum.

Hemingway, P. (1986). Teaching a mixed-level class. *Practical English Teaching, 7*(1), 22.

Hess, N. (2001). *Teaching large multilevel classes.* New York: Cambridge University Press.

Hofstede, G. (1997). *Cultures and organizations: Software of the mind.* New York: McGraw-Hill.

Holec, H. (1981). *Autonomy and foreign language learning.* Oxford: Pergamon Press.

Holliday, A. (2005). *The struggle to teach English as an international language.* Oxford: Oxford University Press.

Hu, R., Chen, G., & Mao, H. (2004). Taking stock of three years of expanded enrollment in higher education. *Chinese Education & Society, 37*(1), 22–35.

Hu, W., & Grove, W. (1991). *Encountering the Chinese.* Yarmouth, ME: Intercultural Press.

Hyland, K. (2003). *Second language writing.* Cambridge: Cambridge University Press.

Impress (Version 3.0) [Computer software]. (2007). OpenOffice.org. http://www .openoffice.org/product/impress.html iTunes (Version 8.1) [Computer software]. (2009). Cupertino, CA: Apple. http://www.apple.com/itunes/download

James, P. (2001). *Teachers in action*. Cambridge: Cambridge University Press.

Jensen, E. (2005). *Teaching with the brain in mind* (2nd ed.). Alexandria, VA: Association for Supervision and Curriculum Development.

Johnson, D. W., Johnson, R. T., & Holubec, E. J. (2002). *Circles of learning: Cooperation in the classroom* (5th ed.). Edina, MN: Interaction.

Jones, L. (2001). *Working in English. Student book*. Cambridge: Cambridge University Press.

Karavas-Doukas, E. (1996). Using attitude scales to investigate teachers' attitudes to the communicative approach. *ELT Journal, 50*, 187–196.

Katchen, K. (1993, April). *Turning the tables: Choose the videos, construct the course*. Paper presented the 27th Annual TESOL Convention and Exhibit, Atlanta, GA. (ERIC Document Reproduction Service No. ED369270)

Kelly, R. (1996). Language counselling for learner autonomy: The skilled helper in self-access language learning. In R. Pemberton, E. Wi, W. Or, & H. Pierson (Eds.), *Taking control: Autonomy in language learning* (pp. 93–113). Hong Kong: Hong Kong University Press.

Kim, Y., & Kim, J. (2005). Teaching a Korean university writing class: Balancing the process and the genre approach. *Asian EFL Journal, 7*(2). Retrieved May 21, 2009, from http://www.asian-efl-journal.com/June_05_yk&jk.pdf

Kindler, A. (2002). *Survey of the states' limited English proficient students and available educational programs and services 1999–2000 summary report*. Washington, DC: U.S. Department of Education.

Kirson, T. (2008). [Review of the Web site *MakeBeliefsComix.com*]. *Essential Teacher, 5*(2), 52.

Kluckhohn, F., & Strodtbeck, F. (1961). *Variations in value orientations*. New York: Row, Peterson.

Ko, J., Schallert, D. L., & Walters, K. (2003). Rethinking scaffolding: Examining negotiation of meaning in an ESL storytelling task. *TESOL Quarterly, 37*, 303–324.

Kobayashi, M. (2003). The role of peer support in ESL students' accomplishment of oral academic tasks. *Canadian Modern Language Review, 59*, 337–368.

Kroll, B. (2001). Considerations for teaching an ESL/EFL writing course. In M. Celce-Murcia (Ed.), *Teaching English as a second or foreign language* (3rd ed., pp. 219–232). Boston: Heinle & Heinle.

Le Roux, J. (2002). Effective educators are culturally competent communicators. *Intercultural Education, 13*, 37–49.

Lee, F. (1994). *The effect on listening comprehension of using television commercials in a Chinese as a second language course.* Unpublished manuscript. (ERIC Document Reproduction Service No. ED386911)

Lee, L., & Sherman, K. (2005). *All-star.* New York: McGraw-Hill.

Lewis, M. (1996). *Using student-centered methods with teacher-centered ESL students* Toronto, Ontario, Canada: Pippin.

LoCastro, V. (2001). Large classes and student learning. *TESOL Quarterly, 35,* 493–496.

Louie, K. (2005). Gathering cultural knowledge: Useful or use with care? In J. Carroll & J. Ryan (Eds.), *Teaching international students: Improving learning for all* (pp. 17–25). London: Routledge.

MacDonald, M. G., Thiravithul, Z. M., Butkulwong, W., & Kednoi, P. (2002). Team English in adolescent large EFL classes. *PASAA: Journal of Language Teaching and Learning in Thailand, 33,* 18–33.

Marlina, R. (2007). *International students' experiences of participation in university tutorials.* Unpublished master's thesis, Monash University, Australia.

Mathews-Aydinli, J., & Van Horne, R. (2006, April). *Promoting the success of multilevel ESL classes: What teachers and administrators can do.* Washington, DC: Center for Adult English Language Acquisition. Retrieved May 15, 2009, from http://www.cal.org/Caela/esl_resources/briefs/multilevel.pdf

Maybin, J., Mercer, N., & Stierer, B. (1992). Scaffolding learning in the classroom. In K. Norman (Ed.), *Thinking voices: The work of the national oracy project* (pp. 186–195). London: Hodder & Stoughton.

McGee, K., & Fujita, T. (2000). Playing the semiotic game: Analyzing and creating TV commercials in an ESL class. *Language Teacher, 24*(6), 17–24.

McKay, S. L. (2003). Teaching English as an international language: The Chilean context. *ELT Journal, 57,* 139–148.

McTighe, J., & Wiggins, G. (2004). *Understanding by design: Professional development workbook.* Alexandria, VA: Association for Supervision and Curriculum Development.

McVicker, C. J. (2007). Comic strips as a text structure for learning to read. *Reading Teacher, 61,* 85–88.

Meyers, C., & Jones, T. B. (1993). *Promoting active learning: Strategies for the college classroom.* San Francisco: Jossey-Bass.

Miller, K. (2003, Fall). English language learners and the No Child Left Behind Act. *Changing Schools, 1,* 8.

Miller, L. (1999). Self-access language learning in primary and secondary schools: The Malaysian experience and the Hong Kong potential. In B. Morrison (Ed.), *Experiments and evaluation in self-access language learning* (pp. 61–72). Hong Kong: Hong Kong Association of Self-Access Learning and Development.

Mohan, B. (1986). *Language and content.* Reading: Addison-Wesley.

Mozzon-McPherson, M. (2000). An analysis of the skills and functions of language learning advisers. *Links & Letters, 7,* 111–126.

Murphy, J., & Stoller, F. L. (2001). Sustained-content language teaching: An emerging definition. *TESOL Journal, 10*(2/3), 3–5.

Murray, G., & Cotterall, S. (2006). *Independent language learning: What's it all about?* Akita, Japan: Akita International University.

Mutoh, N. (1998). Management of large classes. In J. Richards (Ed.), *Teaching in action: Case studies from second language classrooms* (pp. 35–40). Alexandria, VA: TESOL.

Muzychenko, O. (2007, July). *Learning style variations in a culturally diverse class: A case study.* Paper presented at the Higher Education Research and Development Society at Australasia 30th Annual Conference, Enhancing Higher Education, Theory and Scholarship, Adelaide, Australia.

Myles, J. (2002). Second language writing and research: The writing process and error analysis in student texts. *TESL-EJ, 6*(2), 1–20. Retrieved May 21, 2009, from http://tesl-ej.org/ej22/a1.html

National Board for Professional Teaching Standards. (2008). *The five core propositions.* Retrieved May 21, 2009, from http://www.nbpts.org/the_standards/the_five_core_propositio

National Center for Education Statistics. (1997). *1993–94 schools and staffing survey: A profile of policies and practices for limited English proficient students: Screening methods, program support, and teacher training.* Washington, DC: U.S. Department of Education, Office of Educational Research and Improvement.

National Center for Education Statistics. (2002). *Schools and staffing survey, 1999–2000: Overview of the data for public, private, public charter, and Bureau of Indian Affairs elementary and secondary schools.* Washington, DC: Author. Retrieved September 18, 2009, from http://nces.ed.gov/pubs2002/2002313.pdf

Nelson, G. (1995). Cultural differences in learning styles. In J. M. Reid (Ed.), *Learning styles in the ESL/EFL classroom* (pp. 3–18). Boston: Heinle & Heinle.

Omaggio-Hadley, A. (1993). *Teaching language in context* (2nd ed.). Boston: Heinle & Heinle.

Ong, W. J. (1982). *Orality and literacy: The technologizing of the word.* London: Methuen.

Oshima, A., & Hogue, A. (1997). *An introduction to academic writing.* New York: Addison-Wesley Longman.

Ouyang, H. (2004). *Remaking of face and community of practices: An ethnographic study of what ELT reform means to local and expatriate teachers in today's China.* Beijing, China. Peking University Press.

Ovando, C., Collier, V., & Combs, M. (2003). *Bilingual and ESL classrooms: Teaching in multicultural contexts* (3rd ed.). Boston: McGraw-Hill.

Oxford, R., Massey, R., & Anand, S. (2005). Transforming teacher-student style relationships: Toward a more welcoming and diverse classroom discourse. In J. Frodesen & C. Holten (Eds.), *The power of context in language teaching and learning* (pp. 249–266). Boston: Thomson Heinle.

Pally, M. (Ed.). (2000). *Sustained content-based teaching in academic ESL/EFL: A practical approach.* Boston: Houghton Mifflin.

Palmer, J. C. (1999). Teaching large, heterogeneous classes in ESP. *IATEFL ESP SIG Newsletter, 14.* Retrieved May 17, 2009, from http://www.unav.es/espSig/palmer14.html

Parry, K. J., & Su, X. (Eds.). (1998). *Culture, literacy, and learning English: Voices from the Chinese classroom.* Portsmouth, NH: Heinemann.

Penaflorida, A. H. (2002). Nontraditional forms of assessment and response to student writing: A step toward learner autonomy. In J. C. Richards & W. A. Renandya (Eds.), *Methodology in language teaching: An anthology of current practice* (pp. 344–353). Cambridge: Cambridge University Press.

Peng, N. (2007). Strategies in teaching English to large classes in the universities. *US-China Education, 4*(1), 66–69.

Phan, L. H. (2008). *Teaching English as an international language: Identity, resistance, and negotiation.* Clevedon, England: Multilingual Matters.

Pierre, F. (2005). *Peer interaction in the Haitian public school context.* Unpublished manuscript, School for International Training, Brattleboro, VT.

Poon, A. (1992). *Action research: A study on using TV news to improve listening proficiency* (Research report No. 14). Unpublished manuscript, City Polytechnic of Hong Kong. Retrieved May 17, 2009, from http://www.eric.ed.gov/ERICWebPortal/contentdelivery/servlet/ERICServlet?accno=ED375607

Renaud, S., Tannenbaum, E., & Stantial, P. (2007). Student-centered teaching in large classes with limited resources. *English Teaching Forum, 45*(3), 12–17, 34.

Richards, J. C. (2001). *Curriculum development in language teaching.* Cambridge: Cambridge University Press.

Richards, J. C., & Rodgers, T. S. (2001). *Approaches and methods in language teaching.* New York: Cambridge University Press.

Richards, S. (1998). *ELT spectrum, 6.* Oxford: Oxford University Press.

Rinvolucri, M. (1986). Strategies for a mixed ability group. *Practical English Teaching, 7*(1), 17.

Rogoff, B. (1994). Developing understanding of the idea of communities of learners. *Mind, Culture, and Activity, 1,* 209–229.

Rose, J. (1997). Mixed ability: An "inclusive" classroom. *English Teaching Professional, 3,* 3–5.

Rose, M. (1983). Remedial writing course: A critique and a proposal. *College English, 45,* 109–128.

Rucinski-Hatch, C. (1996). Grandma Moses meets ESL: Art for speaking and writing activities. *Journal of the Imagination in Language Learning and Teaching, 3.* Retrieved May 20, 2009, from http://www.njcu.edu/cill/vol3/rucinski-hatch.html

Scarcella, R. (2002). Some key factors affecting English learners' development of advanced literacy. In M. J. Schleppegrell & M. C. Colombi (Eds.), *Developing advanced literacy in first and second language* (pp. 209–226). Mahwah, NJ: Lawrence Erlbaum.

Schultz, K. (2003). *Listening: A framework for teaching across differences.* New York: Teachers College Press.

See, J. (2000, July). *An active learning model for teaching college students in Japan.* Paper presented at the Year 2000 Conference, Honolulu, Hawaii.

Seelye, H. N. (1993). *Teaching culture: Strategies for intercultural communication.* Chicago: National Textbook Company.

Seliger, H. W., & Shohamy, E. (1989). *Second language research methods.* Oxford: Oxford University Press.

Sheets, R. H. (1998). A theoretical and pedagogical multicultural match, or unbridled serendipity? *Multicultural Education, 6,* 35–38.

Sheets, R. (2005). *Diversity pedagogy: Examining the role of culture in the teaching-learning process.* New York: Pearson.

Shrum, J. L., & Glisan, E. W. (2005). *Teacher's handbook: Contextualized language instruction* (3rd ed.). Boston: Thomson Heinle.

Smith, A., & Rawley, L. A. (1997). Using TV commercials to teach listening and critical thinking. *Journal of the Imagination in Language Learning and Teaching, 4.* Retrieved May 17, 2009, from http://www.njcu.edu/cill/vol4/smith-rawley.html

Stein, J. (1997). Why teach in groups instead of individualized? *Connections, 7,* 39.

Stewart, E., & Bennett, M. (1991). *American cultural patterns: A cross-cultural perspective.* Yarmouth, ME: Intercultural Press.

Storti, C. (1999). *Figuring foreigners out: A practical guide*. Yarmouth, ME: Intercultural Press.

Thornbury, S. (2003). *Natural English teacher development*. Oxford: Oxford University Press.

Thorndyke, E., & Lorge, I. (1944). *The teacher's word book of 30,000 words.* New York: Teachers' College, Columbia University.

Tournaki, N., & Podell, D. M. (2005). The impact of student characteristics and teacher efficacy on teachers' predictions of student success. *Teaching and Teacher Education, 21*, 299–314.

Trueba, H. (1993). Culture and language: The ethnographic approach to the study of learning environments. In B. Merino, H. Trueba, & F. Samaniego (Eds.), *Language and culture in learning: Teaching Spanish to native speakers of Spanish* (pp. 26–44). London: Falmer Press.

Ur, P. (1996). *A course in language teaching: Practice and theory*. Cambridge: Cambridge University Press.

Vygotsky, L. S. (1978). *Mind in society: The development of higher psychological processes*. Cambridge, MA: Harvard University Press.

Wajnryb, R. (1990). *Grammar dictation*. Oxford: Oxford University Press.

Wenger, E., McDermott, R., & Snyder, W. M. (2002). *Cultivating communities of practice: A guide to managing knowledge*. Boston: Harvard Business School Press.

Williams, J. G. (2003). Providing feedback on ESL students' written assignments. *Internet TESL Journal, 9*(10), 1–5. Retrieved May 21, 2009, from http://iteslj.org/Techniques/Williams-Feedback.html

Wright, A. (1994). *1000+ pictures for teachers to copy*. London: Nelson.

Wright, S., & Lander, D. (2003). Collaborative group interactions of students from two ethnic backgrounds. *Higher Education Research and Development, 22*, 237–252.

Yang, N.-D. (2003). Integrating portfolios into learning strategy-based instruction for EFL college students. *International Review of Applied Linguistics in Language Teaching, 41*, 293–317.

YouTube. (2009). *YouTube*. Retrieved May 18, 2009, from http://www.youtube.com/

Zamel, V. (1985). Responding to student writing. *TESOL Quarterly, 19*, 79–101.

Zemach, D. E. (2003). *College writing: From paragraph to essay*. Oxford: Macmillan.

Zimmerman, B. (2006–2009). *Makebeliefscomix.com*. Retrieved May 20, 2009, from http://makebeliefscomix.com/

Index